Finding Your Counseling Career

Finding Your Counseling Career

Stories, Procedures, and Resources for Career Seekers

BROOKE B. COLLISON

Routledge
Taylor & Francis Group
New York   London

Routledge
Taylor & Francis Group
270 Madison Avenue
New York, NY 10016

Routledge
Taylor & Francis Group
27 Church Road
Hove, East Sussex BN3 2FA

Printed in the United States of America on acid-free paper
10 9 8 7 6 5 4 3 2 1

International Standard Book Number: 978-0-415-80039-6 (Hardback) 978-0-415-80040-2 (Paperback)

Library of Congress Cataloging-in-Publication Data

Collison, Brooke B.
  Finding your counseling career : stories, procedures, and resources for career seekers / Brooke Collison.
      p. cm.
  Includes bibliographical references and index.
  ISBN 978-0-415-80039-6 (hardcover : alk. paper) -- ISBN 978-0-415-80040-2 (pbk. : alk. paper)
  1. Counseling--Vocational guidance. I. Title.

BF636.64.C65 2010
158'.3023--dc22

2009053735

Visit the Taylor & Francis Web site at
http://www.taylorandfrancis.com

and the Routledge Web site at
http://www.routledgementalhealth.com

I appreciate the encouragement of my spouse, Joan, throughout the process of writing this book. I also appreciate the contributions that Nancy Garfield made, even though she was not able to write chapters for this edition. I particularly appreciate the willingness of the 14 people I interviewed for the profile section. And I appreciate the interviewees all giving me permission to use their names and their places of work in order to give the profiles a firm touch of reality for you, the reader. Thanks to all of you.

BBC
Corvallis, Oregon

CONTENTS

PART III

PART IV

PREFACE

This book, *Finding Your Counseling Career,* comes as the third generation of a project that began several years ago with my colleague, Dr. Nancy Garfield. Earlier volumes, entitled *Careers in Counseling and Human Services* (American Association for Counseling and Development, 1990) and *Careers in Counseling and Human Development* (Taylor & Francis, 1996), were collections of chapters written by a set of experts, each of whom could speak to the kinds of counseling careers found in different settings—elementary and secondary schools, colleges, business and industry, private practice, rehabilitation settings, and the like.

Dr. Garfield and I worked and taught courses together when we were both at Wichita State University, Kansas. We share a common philosophy about the way that people make decisions to enter one of the human service professions. We both believe there was more unknown than known about the counseling fields that people were considering, and we wanted a book for students that would give them both an introduction to different human service professions as well as suggestions about their decision-making process.

The second book, *Careers in Counseling and Human Services,* was published by Taylor & Francis. Dr. Garfield and I thought we had finished our work. We also thought that the book would have a fairly short life because it contained information that was, to some extent, time limited. We included some salary information and resource lists for readers, with address lists for readers to use to send mail requests.

Whether it was fortunate or unfortunate, the book remained active on the Taylor & Francis sales list long after the time that Dr. Garfield and I thought that it would. When we received copies of sales reports, both of us would suggest that it was time to retire the publication. We sent our requests to Dana Bliss, with Taylor & Francis, who usually responded that if we thought that the book was out of date, we should write a new and updated version. Bliss was persuasive, and this volume is the result.

Dr. Garfield contributed significantly to the concepts presented in this volume. We had several long conversations at the bookstore where she now works part-time in her retirement. Health issues have prevented her from being an active writer, but she developed significant ideas about how to make this book less dated than the earlier volumes.

There are several major differences between this volume and the earlier titles. The book comes out of my computer rather than being a collection of contributed chapters. The book does not include current salary data for occupational titles but does include Internet search procedures for those who want to find salary information. The book includes more exercises and self-tests for the interested reader who wishes to explore personal characteristics and how they fit with the counseling professions.

One totally new concept in this volume is the section that includes profiles of persons who were initially in counseling positions but who have moved to different professional positions. The core element is that they continue to use their counseling skills. The idea for this section is one that emerged during conversations with Dr. Garfield, and, I must be frank, it is the element that piqued my interest enough to agree to Bliss's request that we produce an updated volume.

Dr. Garfield and I agreed that the majority of books on career decision making tend to stop with entry into the initial career of interest. When we reviewed our first two volumes, we discovered that chapter writers might describe the educational process to be licensed in a particular field and then describe the job functions of a person in that field, but that was the end of their discussion. There were no extensions of the career path beyond the entry level. We both knew that for many persons in the helping professions, there is a rich life that might follow their initial entry. School counselors move on to become school administrators or college professors, counseling psychologists might leave private practice and open a consulting business, and counselors join businesses that provide services to various counseling groups or clients. The opportunity to interview people who had made such moves and be able to then present a small snapshot of their career changes and the decision processes that went into those changes posed an intriguing element that we wanted to include.

I became so involved with the value of the interviews and profiles that I strongly urge readers to follow the same process in their own career search. The concept of informational interviews is not new. I rediscovered their value as I prepared this manuscript, and when people would ask how my writing was going, my typical response would be to say that I was excited about the new element—interviews and profiles. I will have more to say about this process in the last section of the book. I hope that the results from the interviews and profiles are valuable to you. I also hope that you will get caught up in the value of the process and will conduct your own interviews.

I

The first section of this book contains four chapters that set the stage for you, the reader, to begin your process of finding your way. Whether you are not certain about a career in one of the counseling professions or if you are absolutely certain exactly what kind of counseling professional you want to be in the future, I hope that these four chapters will provide you with information leading to more certainty about your decision.

Chapter 1, "Finding Your Way," begins to suggest a process of self-examination and questioning about you and potential career decisions you might make. The chapter will encourage you to enlist the aid of others who can provide additional perspective to who you are and what characteristics you have that do or do not fit one of the counseling professions.

The chapter provides a general interactive framework leading to the self-portrait described above. The chapter will also introduce concepts such as educational preparation for one of the counseling professions. It will include the first of several discussions of licensing and certification so central to the counseling professions. It will also include a preliminary discussion of program accreditation—one means of letting you know if the preparation program you are considering is a quality program or not.

Chapter 2, "Is a Counseling Career for You?" digs deeper into the topic of self-examination. The chapter includes several kinds of questions for discussion, checklists, and rating scales for you and for others to use. A set of personal characteristics will be presented in a form you can use in discussion with others—whether they are fellow students, family, friends, or professionals who know you well. The chapter title continues the question present throughout this book of helping you decide if being one of the counseling professionals is really the appropriate choice for you.

Chapter 3, "Counselor Characteristics," is built around a list of characteristics thought to be essential for persons in one of the counseling professions. The list provided in the chapter is not comprehensive—it would take a much longer book than this one to include and discuss every characteristic thought to be essential for good counselors. In fact, you will find, as in Chapter 2, that there is not a set of absolutes you must meet in order to match the characteristics of a good counselor. The list in Chapter 3 will give you much opportunity for self-reflection, discussion, and interaction as you continue to find your way.

Chapter 4, "Preparation," focuses on what it means to be in a preparation program to become a counselor. Because nearly all counselor preparation programs exist at the graduate level, there are several discussions about the nature of graduate school, admission, background preparation, and program selection that you may want to keep in mind for your career decision making. This chapter suggests ways you can determine if the preparation program will actually lead you to your chosen career.

Throughout all of these chapters, and in the rest of the book, you will be encouraged to seek information from a variety of sources. One of the most common procedures suggested will be to do informational interviews with persons in some professional position or in an educational program that relates to the decision or decisions you are in the process of making. The book will tell you that the quality of the data collected through informational interviews is dependent on the nature of the person being interviewed, the kind of questions you ask, and the way you process the interview data. Interviewing one person who is a poor example of the career you are interested in and who is burned out and generally out of sorts in many ways will give you a distorted picture. Although emphasized as valuable, informational interviews have their built-in problems, and you must exercise caution and good judgment in their use.

1

FINDING YOUR WAY

Is your perfect career opportunity waiting for you in the field of counseling or in another of the human service opportunities? If so, will you wait until it finds you? Or, will you begin an active search to find that perfect career possibility—and, further, will you begin to prepare yourself to be the very best qualified applicant for that position when the time comes to move out of the educational and preparation stage and into your chosen position? This book will help you decide what that career opportunity looks like and then walk you through the steps of self-examination and testing that will let you know with more certainty that your choice is right for you—it will help you find your way.

The picture painted in the paragraph above—of an ideal job "out there" which finds you—is far less likely than a process during which you make decisions about yourself and actively prepare yourself for a position that you seek. This book will explore several components of that process. You will have an opportunity to examine yourself and do some deciding about the extent to which you fit the field of counseling or human service careers. You will look at the different kinds of preparation programs that exist for people entering the sort of career you envision for yourself. You will take a look at the kinds of certification and licensing processes that are attached to positions like the one (or ones) you aspire to hold. You will take a look at various strategies for entering the employment arena. And finally, you will be able to look at the lives of several people who have entered one of the counseling professions and then have moved on to other related kinds of professional positions but who continue to utilize the knowledge and skill sets they acquired for their initial counseling or human service job.

The phrase, "counseling or human service profession," is a mouthful. In this book, the word *counseling* will be used to cover a pretty wide variety of professional career or occupational titles. Where it is necessary, other specific job titles will be used, but, for the most part, counseling will be used whether we are talking about school counselors, mental health counselors, university counseling center professionals, rehabilitation counselors, or others. If the discussion is about a position that has a license attached to the title (e.g., school psychologist or licensed clinical social worker), then those titles will be used. In other respects, those titles will be subsumed under the label "counselor" for ease of reading (and writing).

Throughout this book, you will have numerous opportunities to do some *self testing* or exploration on topics or issues that relate to the overall topic. There will be three kinds of self-test offered—some will be questions for you to ponder and provide your own answer; some will be questions or situations where I will suggest that you obtain information from other people about you or some aspect of a topic under discussion; and some will be suggestions about activities you could undertake in order to test some component of a counseling career. More will be presented about each of those later.

You can choose to do or not do the self-test and suggested activities (unless an instructor makes completion of one of the activities part of a class assignment with a grade attached). It is up to you whether you do the activity or not, and that leaves you totally in control of using the activity or not, the integrity you bring to the activity, the extent to which you disclose or discuss the activity with anyone else, and, ultimately, the value of the activity for you in making the kind of decisions this book assumes you are facing.

As an example, if an activity asks, "To what extent do you describe yourself as needing to control other people's behavior?" you can quickly say to yourself (or someone else), "I'm not controlling at all—I'm very accepting," even if you know that unless things go your way you get really upset with people and that you often find ways to make sure that people do what you want rather than accept something that is more important to them. No one is going to challenge your self-description unless you share your self-assessment with others in an atmosphere where open discussion, accurate feedback, and honesty are the norm. Short of that kind of growth environment, I urge you to be honest and frank with yourself as you read through the various exercises and self-assessments in this book. In nearly every instance, there will not be right or wrong answers. There will be a lot of stimulus questions, thought provokers, and opportunities for thinking and reflection.

I suppose there are some questions that come closer to having right and wrong answers than others. For example, if you are planning to become a counselor in some setting, a question such as, "Do you see yourself as a people person?" has a pretty transparent right answer. It is possible, in some settings, I suppose, to not like people and still become a counselor who might get positive reviews from others; however, that scenario is rather difficult to imagine. I recall a friend once talking about his daughter and saying, "She wants to be a social worker among the affluent and well adjusted." He chuckled as he said it, but there was some semblance of truth in his statement because his daughter had a difficult time being among or working among persons who seemed to be on a lower socioeconomic scale, and she frequently expressed dislike for people whose behavior displayed any hint at anything other than a well-adjusted, happy, productive, and satisfied life. In the end, she did not enter one of the helping professions.

The second major section of this book will suggest a number of different activities designed to give you a broad base of knowledge about different career options in counseling or other human service occupations. You may be familiar with *shadowing* activities where you follow a person around for a period of time and try to decide if what they do is something you would want to do as a career. Another form of information gathering related to career searching is often described as *informational interviewing*—activities where you conduct focused interviews with one or more persons who hold the kind of position you are considering.

Shadowing and informational interviews are both activities that are highly dependent on the person you are shadowing or interviewing and the extent to which you are able to process the information you obtain from the activities. In short, if you shadow someone in a job who is a poor example of how the job could be performed or if they are tired and burned out and only grumble about what they *have* to do, then the experience can be disastrous unless your own processing—by yourself or with others—lets you examine that person's view of the world and understand that it is only one view. The experience can still be very valuable for you in making your own decisions about the particular human services career you were shadowing if you can identify what it is in that person's world that has led to the condition expressed in what you observed. You may be able to do another form of self-assessment and determine if you would react the same way in the same position—was it the nature of the position or the nature of the person, which resulted in you seeing someone who was disgruntled, unhappy, doing poor work, or whatever you observed.

Neither shadowing nor informational interviews must be with the absolute perfect models of professional behavior in the most ideal of situations (that may be difficult to find, anyway). The data resulting from shadowing or interviewing need to be processed in an effective manner for the best results for you. Informational interviewing is also highly dependent on the questions you ask. Like shadowing, informational interviews are a means to collecting data which you can use to assess how well you fit or do not fit in that professional setting. The quality of your results also depends on the quality of the processing that follows the interview. If you are reading this book by yourself, then I urge you to seek out persons who can provide a third ear or an additional look or a different perspective on what you are learning about yourself and others.

Of course, there are many print and nonprint forms of information you can tie to your process of learning about different occupational situations. The Internet can provide huge amounts of information. I will suggest various sources throughout this book; however, I am less likely to give you a specific Web address for material than I am to guide the words you might use in an Internet search process. Web addresses may change over time, making anything specific out of date quickly. The general search paths to find information will be similar over time—and that is what I will suggest to you.

Nearly all of the counseling positions you might consider require specialized education or preparation programs. There are some general guidelines for selecting an educational program, which are more likely to lead you to the counseling position you seek. It is important to understand how educational programs relate to certification or licensing for different counseling positions. It is also important to understand how education programs are accredited and how you can determine if the program you are interested in meets the criteria necessary to assist you in getting to that ideal job.

You may have noticed that I used first-person pronouns thus far in this book. I will continue to do that and will share some personal experiences and observations of my own in the different sections. The observations come from a long career in education, counseling, and teaching about counseling. I will also include illustrations and comments about people I have worked with over the years.

In the last section of this book, there will be several profiles of people who completed a preparation program in counseling and worked as a counselor for some time. Then, for a variety of reasons, they moved on to a different occupation; however, they continue to use the knowledge and skill they acquired for their initial counseling position. In the words of one of the persons I interviewed for this section, "Counselor education was the best preparation for a job I never thought I'd have." The people profiled in that section of the book are named and their work setting is named—each gave approval to use their name and work setting after reading the profile I wrote following our interviews. I must add a personal note here—conducting the interviews and writing the profiles was very enjoyable for me. It was a delight to see the different kinds of jobs that people held, how they acquired those jobs, what they enjoy and do not enjoy about them, and how their counselor preparation and counselor experience fit with their current work. That is one of the reasons that I urge you to do as many informational interviews as possible as you work through this book and consider your own occupational future.

2

IS A COUNSELING CAREER FOR YOU?

Are you the kind of person who would make a good counselor? Do you have the essential characteristics, skills, and personal makeup to become a mental health worker, a human service professional, a psychologist, or any of the other professional occupations that this book describes? You probably have some belief that you are a fit for one of those professions or you might not be reading this far. On the other hand, if you have some questions or doubts about the goodness of fit of a career in one of the counseling fields for you, then the next chapters will help you take a look at who you are and how you might fit in a counseling career. Whether you have a solid conviction that it is the right career choice or you are very uncertain, the questions, activities, and discussions that follow should give you some food for thought—and perhaps put you in a place to feel much better about your career decision (regardless of what it might be).

The obvious first question to ask is, "Are you a people person?" One of the very simple systems for describing occupations is to classify them as dealing with "people, data, or things." It is very simplistic, but it is a good place to start.

All of the counseling careers would be classified as "people" occupations; however, there are aspects of each that deal to some extent with both data and things. We will set those aside for now and just think about people.

I will assume for a moment that you describe yourself as a "people person." To take this to some other levels:

1. What kind of people person are you?
2. How would others describe you on the people-person dimension?
3. What part of being a people person is difficult for you?
4. What part of being a people person is most rewarding?

The first question—"What kind of people person are you?"—may appear a little strange, but it is a serious issue to explore. Are you the kind of person who walks into a room and everyone notices that you entered? In a conversation with one or two other people, are you most likely to be the one who chooses topics and others follow your lead in contributing to the discussion? Are you the one who would go out of the way to make certain that a stranger who entered the room was introduced to everyone and made to feel comfortable?

Might you be a person who is rather quiet in a group but who notices what everyone is doing and saying? If someone in the group is being very quiet, would you be inclined to ask them something to get them started in the conversation or would you be comfortable letting them also be a quiet listener?

What do you do if the topic is uninteresting or if people are talking about subjects that make you uncomfortable—perhaps telling jokes that you believe are inappropriate or making sexist or racist references? Would you speak up to correct their behavior or would you let them go on under the belief that it is not your business to speak up?

And what do you do if you are in direct conflict with a person or with more than one person in a group? Do you find that you are avoiding the topic and the persons in order to not be in the middle of a conflict? Or are you more likely to push back in a verbal fashion in order to defend your position?

What sort of interactions with people make you uncomfortable? What kind of interaction with people gives you the most satisfaction? And what kinds of interactions or subjects do you find that you work to avoid because they would just be too unpleasant for you to deal with?

Wow! That is a lot of questions—and you may be wondering which set of answers would more likely point the way for you to feel confident that a career in counseling would be best for you. Unfortunately, there is no single, perfect set of characteristics most descriptive of a counselor. You might answer the questions one way and a friend another, and both of you could be good counselor material; however, let's take a look inside some of the issues above and see how they might relate to a counseling career.

Skip to the end of this chapter and study the list entitled "What Kind of People Person Are You?" Take some time now and mark your responses. You may want to copy the page and make extra copies for other persons or you might want to mark the page in order to give you feedback or to have in hand for discussion time. Do not try to fill out the page quickly—take your time and return to the page from time to time after you had a chance to think about your responses.

HOW DO OTHERS SEE YOU?

Now that you made a few statements about the kind of person you believe you are, it is time to do a little "checking" with others. You can do this a couple of different ways: (a) take the "What Kind of a People Person Are You?" sheet that you filled out to one or more people who know you or who have had a chance to observe you in group situations and ask them about the way you marked your sheet; or (b) give a blank check sheet to one or more people who know you and ask them to mark how they see you on each of the dimensions on the sheet.

The next step, obviously, is to sit down with the other persons—either one at a time or in a small group—and have a good discussion about the way your markings are similar or different. Note—I am not saying for you to see if they marked "right" or "wrong." Remember, this exercise is about perceptions of the way you are, not if you scored a particular way. Previously, I wrote that there is no ideal profile for a person who plans to enter one of the counseling professions—even though there are some rather obvious indicators.

If you and another person have very discrepant markings, do not enter the discussion with statements indicating that you believe the other person is correct or not. And the other person should not try to convince you that you have marked one of the continua incorrectly. Instead, you might extend the discussion with a set of exploratory questions:

> "Will you share your perceptions of me based on the way you marked the sheet?"
> "What did you see which suggests that I am a 'quiet person'" (or any of the other descriptors on the sheet)?
> "Can you give me an example of 'a time I changed the subject'" (or any of the other descriptors on the sheet)?

Your response to any of the observations or perceptions shared by another person (or persons) you are talking with should be to listen to those perceptions, try to determine how they fit your own image of the way you are, and seek to understand what other people are experiencing with you that leads them to the statements they share with you. Your response should not be to refute the comments. It is not a time to make defensive comments to another about what you are hearing, but it is a good time to keep track of your own reactions to what you hear—do the statements you hear from others tend to make you feel defensive? Does what you hear make you want to convince the other person that he or she is wrong? In the same way, do you feel compelled to tell another person that he or she is correct in their perceptions of you—especially if the perception being shared is one that you believe is supportive of a career choice in one of the counseling fields?

Once you have had time to share perceptions with each other, you might enter a second stage of dialogue. This stage would let you express feelings about what you heard. For example,

> "Hearing you say that I tend to change the subject frequently makes me uncomfortable."
> "It feels good to know that people see me as someone who helps others feel comfortable in new or strange situations."
> "I'm puzzled by the comments that I avoid conflict."

These statements are the kind that let you express how and what you are feeling about what you have heard rather than putting you in a confrontational posture of disagreeing with a statement or of telling a person that he or she has made an error in observation. The opportunity to do that may come later in the discussion (if there is enough time), but it is not the most productive component of this exercise that is designed to compare the way you see yourself and the way other people see you on a few dimensions of what kind of people person you are.

The information you provide about yourself and the information you receive from others should all be considered data that you put in your own decision process about whether you are the kind of person who could become good at one of the counseling professions. Remember, information is just that until you place some kind of value statement on that information and it turns into something positive or negative for you.

DIFFICULTIES

There are a lot of things that can become difficult in any of the counseling or helping professions. Counselors hear and see and are expected to work with people and issues that make many uncomfortable just knowing about them. Counselors work with people in distress, in conflict, who have experienced loss, who are not able to make decisions, and on and on. So, one of the major questions you must ask yourself as you consider one or more of the counseling professions is, "What part of being a people person is difficult for you?"

This question again asks you to take a hard look at yourself and to do an assessment of characteristics that may have more or less to do with one of the counseling professions. For example, you may be a person who is uncomfortable in large groups. Does that mean that you should or should not go into one of the counseling professions? No. Many counselors work by themselves in private practice or they have only two or three colleagues with whom they interact on a daily basis. Being uncomfortable in a crowd may not seem to have anything to do with a match with one of the counseling professions. Awareness that you are uncomfortable in a crowd may suggest that you dig a little deeper and be able to answer the question, "What is it about being in a crowd that makes you uncomfortable?" Depending on the answer to the "cause" question, you may have more information to put in your "appropriate-for-counseling" decision. Does the discomfort come from a general dislike for people? If so, then counseling may not be a good career choice. If the discomfort comes from your inability to be in control of what is going on or the likelihood that someone else might make a statement you consider offensive, then there is less that suggests that counseling is not a good choice and more that suggests there are other issues for you to examine about your own beliefs and behaviors.

Remember that what you are really exploring are the kinds of personal interactions that are difficult for you. They might be situations where you feel a little ill at ease or you might think of times when you have been anxious about a situation or event—giving a speech in front of a class or being tested on something when you did not feel totally prepared. Each of those bits of information contributes to the total picture of what you know about yourself with respect to people. They describe things about you related to being a people person. It is up to you to decide the meaning for the experiences you have had.

REWARDING SITUATIONS

You should spend as much time thinking about the various rewarding situations you experienced as you would those that have made you uncomfortable.

How would you finish the sentence, "I feel best when I am in _____ situation(s) with other people."

Or, "When do I feel most comfortable in people situations?"

Another aspect of this dimension is related to something we often do not like to admit—what kind of people do you like best and what kind of people do you dislike? If *dislike* is too strong a word, then what kind of people do you know that you intentionally avoid? For example, if you are conscientious about your diet and value being in good physical shape and good health, you might know that you avoid people who are obese. Conversely, if you are obese, you may find that you avoid skinny people. Or, you may know that you do not go out of your way to be close to people of a particular racial group. Your discomfort may be triggered by persons much older than you are. On the opposite side of this issue is the possibility that each of those groups I have just named may be groups or individuals with whom you have very rewarding experiences.

Take a hard look at your people likes and dislikes. Draw a line down the center of a page making two vertical columns. On one side, label it "likes" and label the other column "dislikes." Keep the sheet near you and from time to time add persons or groups to the left or right column. Do not try to do it in just one sitting—this kind of activity is better done if you keep the task in front of you and as things or situations occur to you, you become aware of "that's another one for the left (or right) column."

A note of caution: This is not the kind of page you want in just anyone's hands. There may be entries on your page that require some explaining for some people, particularly if you have identified racial, ethnic, or other stereotypical groups in either your "like" or "dislike" columns.

If just two columns—like and dislike—are too few to really give you a chance to explore aspects of yourself, then make a three- or four-column page. Create your own labels for each column: "very comfortable," "comfortable," "uncomfortable," "very uncomfortable," or "approach," "avoid," "mixed." You develop the labels that will help you develop the best data for your decision making. If you enter specific names in some of the columns, remember that your data sheet might be hard to explain if other people see it without explanation. If you have said that "Jane" is in the "very uncomfortable" column, how will you explain that to Jane?

The point of the exercise is to continue to build information about yourself, which you can use for the larger decision about deciding your own appropriateness for being in one of the counseling professions. I urge you to continue to work through the other questions and suggestions for self-study. I hope you can maintain an open approach to what your future might become and how some kind of counseling profession might fit in that future. It will be particularly helpful if you can focus on those characteristics, topics, or issues where your self perception differs from the perception of others. Of course, the only way you would know if a difference exists is to have the kind of relationship with one or more persons where you can dialogue and obtain that information. Good wishes.

WHAT KIND OF PEOPLE PERSON ARE YOU?

Put an "X" on the line to indicate where you believe you are on the continuum.

When I enter a room, people generally notice me.

YES   **Don't Know**   NO

In a conversation with one or two other people, I tend to initiate topics.

YES   **Don't Know**   NO

I will go out of my way to make certain that a stranger gets introduced to others.

YES   **Don't Know**   NO

I will make certain that strangers feel comfortable in a group I am in.

YES   **Don't Know**   NO

I tend to be rather quiet in a group.

YES   **Don't Know**   NO

I notice and am aware of what is going on with others in a group.

YES   **Don't Know**   NO

I will work to get silent members involved in a conversation in a group.

YES   **Don't Know**   NO

I am comfortable letting silent persons remain silent in a group.

YES   **Don't Know**   NO

If the topic of conversation is uninteresting, I'll manage to change the subject.

YES   **Don't Know**   **NO**

If people in a group are making insensitive comments—racial or ethnic, for example—I will either change the subject or leave.

YES   **Don't Know**   **NO**

If people in a group are making insensitive comments, I will challenge them.

YES   **Don't Know**   **NO**

If I experience conflict with a person in conversation, I tend to be silent about it.

YES   **Don't Know**   **NO**

Write three topics of conversation which tend to make you uncomfortable.

Write two kinds of interactions with others which give you the most satisfaction.

Write an example of an interaction that made you uncomfortable.

3

COUNSELOR CHARACTERISTICS

Now that you have begun to look at your own characteristics and have completed several exercises to help you develop data about yourself as a people person, take a look at some of the more specific characteristics associated with being a counselor. The following list includes descriptors or characteristics that many people in the counseling professions would identify as very important:

- Be a good listener.
- Be open-minded.
- Be able to hear strong emotions expressed.
- Be able to let people make their own decisions.
- Be positive and optimistic about possibilities.
- Be able to work without specific reinforcement or recognition.
- Be interested in and able to work with many different populations.
- Be empathetic without getting "hooked" by another's situation.
- Be aware of your own boundaries and be able to maintain them.
- Be able to take care of your own physical, emotional, and mental well-being.
- Be intellectually curious and a continuing learner.

The list above is not comprehensive. There are other characteristics that could be added depending on the kind of counseling philosophy you take on as your own and depending on the kind of counselor or the kind of counseling setting in which you work. If we examine each of the items in the list above, some of the explanation for each would be as follows.

BE A GOOD LISTENER

Listening is the most common component of every counseling philosophy or counseling practice. Whether counselors work with one client at a time or with a group of people, the most important job for the counselor is to listen and find ways to make certain that the speakers know they are heard and understood.

There are many kinds of listening exercises instructors may use in course work in counseling. When you were young, you might have played the game (sometimes called "Gossip") where people sit in a circle and one person whispers a short, simple statement to the person on either the right or left of him or her. That person whispers the same statement to the person next to him or her, and this continues until it gets to the last person in the circle who says the statement out loud for the group. Inevitably, the original statement does not resemble the final statement; if the group is large, people in the group will claim that neither the original nor the final statements were the ones whispered to them and passed along to their neighbor. In fact, there will usually be many variations of the original statement expressed by people in the group. Although this may be a typical party game played by young people, it illustrates one of the common problems in day-to-day communication—it is difficult for people to hear with accuracy and then repeat what they have heard.

Counselors must be able to accurately hear what clients say. A frequent complaint about interpersonal communication is the lack of listening and the subsequent lack of understanding. Think of the number of times you have heard people say, "No one listens to me," or "No one understands me." It does not have to be teens or young people who make these statements—the topic is a common focus of situation comedy on television and an almost constant theme of jokes and content for comedians. Stories about marital conflict often have as their core issue the condition that one partner either does not listen to the other, or if there is some listening, that it is not interpreted accurately and a great confusion or conflict results.

Counselors must be able to listen with accuracy. Counselors frequently talk about being able to hear not only what the person says, but what they are feeling. This is described as listening with accurate empathy—the ability to connect with and understand what another person is feeling emotionally without becoming personally caught up in those emotions to the point that counselors lose their own identity in the process. This does not mean that counselors cannot or do not feel along with what the client is feeling, but counselors must have enough understanding of themselves that they do not become enmeshed with the clients they work with.

One question you can ask yourself to test out an important aspect of listening is, "Can I listen to another person's story without having to tell my own?" If you listen to the conversations of other people (including your own conversations), you will frequently find that a person may begin to tell something important about themselves only to have one of the listeners break in with a related story of his or her own. The result of this exchange is that the original storyteller has had the focus jerked away from him or her. When this happens in counseling, it is very destructive of the counseling relationship. Sadly enough, when it does occur, many people are so polite that they will not call the interrupter to task by letting the interrupter know he or she has committed a listening sin.

Young people often lack that socialized politeness and will point out the listener's error. Some years ago one of my graduate students was in my building with her young son—perhaps about 6 or 7 years old. I enjoy small children, so it was easy to lean down to his level and engage him in conversation. It was not a counseling session, but I would always hope that my conversations use my better counseling skills. I asked him how old he was, where he went to school, what grade he was in, and about what it was like to be with his mother at her school. Then I asked, "What grade are you in?" and he immediately said, "I already told you that." A more polite formally socialized adult is less likely to do what the young boy did. What I had done is illustrate to him that I was not listening as well as I should have. At least, I was not remembering very well. I think he was turned off by my repeating a question, and he turned away from me to find some other more interesting activity.

During the course of counselor preparation, students will be involved in many listening exercises—active listening, paraphrasing exercises, reflection of affect, and others. The framework on which most of these skills are built is your ability to be a good listener just by being who you are. It is another fundamental skill that you need to consciously assess and work to improve on your own and with the help of others.

BE OPEN-MINDED

Clients in counseling situations frequently bring value-laden issues to the counselor. An essential characteristic of good counselors is that they are open-minded about the things they hear from others. This does not mean that counselors agree with every position they hear from clients or others, but it does mean that counselors can listen and have a degree of understanding of what they hear without having to impose their own views or values on the clients they serve.

Value conflicts for counselors center around some of the most personally important issues or beliefs we have as human beings—the value of life, issues of sexual expression, religious practice, gender equity, and so on. A question frequently posed for counselors in training is, "To what extent do your own values and beliefs help or hinder your ability to be a good counselor?"

Graduate students in counseling frequently struggle with value-conflict issues. Those very strong beliefs emerge in statements they might make such as, "I could never be a counselor for a person who...." You might think of what kind of person or what kind of personal behavior would fill in the blank of that sentence for yourself. To recognize that you have such strong value differences with a person or a group that you know you could not be an effective counselor with them does not mean that you are not open-minded—it means that you are aware enough of your own values and beliefs to know where you could and could not be effective in certain situations.

A different kind of closed-mindedness in counseling comes for the person who has a very strong set of values or beliefs and sees counseling as a way to promote those values and beliefs to others. Consider, for example, a person who has a strong religious orientation and sees counseling as an opportunity to persuade others to take up that same religious orientation, or a person who is in recovery and active in a program such as Alcoholics Anonymous who sees every individual in need of a 12-Step program. You can probably make a list of other potential value situations that could easily become a cause for counselors—issues surrounding abortion, use of drugs, treatment of children, sex before or outside of marriage, homosexuality, attending college, divorce, choice of certain occupations, and so on.

In counselor preparation programs, value and belief issues will be discussed, and counselors can find ways to reconcile their personal positions with counseling practice. Some theorists suggested that it is impossible for counselors to practice "value free," but it is possible to practice "value fair." Counselors often use mechanisms such as printed statements about their own beliefs so that potential clients know in advance what that counselor's value position is regarding the kind of issues named above. It certainly would be unethical and unprofessional to be a counselor who subtly and without openly advising such actively works to persuade a client to adopt a particular position or to take a specific course of action just because it is what the counselor would do. You may have heard people make statements to the effect that because of some experience they had, they intend to become a counselor in order to help others with that same experience. Although this is not totally inappropriate in every situation, it does become inappropriate when the experience becomes your singular mission in life.

The question you must be asking yourself at this time is whether you are aware enough of your own values and beliefs that you could decide if you could be a good, open-minded listener in a counseling situation. If you have questions about that, then further exploration of your own values and beliefs would be an essential exercise. Even if you think you have a good understanding of your own values and beliefs, continued exploration of what those are and how they would affect a counseling relationship is something that always requires constant attention. If you see yourself entering one of the counseling professions in order to promote a particular set of values or beliefs, then I would encourage you to consider other areas of study.

A phrase that has long been a standard in counselor preparation is, "Counselor, Know Thyself." That certainly applies to the areas of values and beliefs.

BE ABLE TO HEAR STRONG EMOTIONS EXPRESSED

Counselors often hear people tell powerful stories about themselves, their families, their work or school situations, accidents, impending illness, critical decisions, family trauma, or any of the thousands of events or conditions that can bring a counselor and a client together. In those counseling situations, people express every feeling or emotion known to exist—and often those expressions are forceful, with tears at sadness or distress, yelling from anger or frustration, or silence from being immobilized by the load of the human condition.

One of the great gifts that counselors bring to their clients is the ability to listen, hear, and accept the strong emotion the client expresses without the counselor turning away or leaving because it is too much for him or her to bear. Counselors must be able to hear strong emotions expressed.

As you consider your own preparation for one of the counseling fields, it is essential to examine what you know about yourself in relation to both the expression of strong emotion and the observer–listener– acceptor of strong emotion. What do you do when people cry? What do you do when people express anger—either at you or anger about another which they express in your presence? What do you do when people are so depressed they can barely function and may sit silently for long periods of time? It is important to consider these and all other emotional expressions as you enter the counseling field.

It is also important to think about the meaning you attach to the expression of strong emotion from others. If you have grown up with a core belief that, "Men don't cry," what are you going to do the first time a big, strong, athletic-looking guy sits in front of you and weeps buckets of tears? Will you put some meaning on that action that may inhibit your ability to be helpful with him in whatever process he is working on that brought him to your office? Similarly, if your strong value set includes a belief that women do not have anger toward their children, what are you going to do the first time that a mother sits in front of you and describes how furious she is with one or more of her children and that she refuses to have anything to do with him or her because of something that has happened?

I do not suggest that counselors should be comfortable with strong emotion expressed by others. It may never be possible to be comfortable with another person's pain, joy, anger, depression, hurt, confusion, bitterness, or any other emotion expressed. It is possible to be at a stage where you can hear and accept that strong emotion without the emotion distorting your effectiveness.

To reach that point where you can work with strong emotion, you need to do more soul searching. Make a list of every strong emotion you can think of. Think of situations where you have seen the emotion expressed—what did you do? Think of situations where you have wanted to express that emotion or you have, in fact, expressed that emotion—what happened to you and to the others who expressed it? Can you identify kinds of emotion where it would be helpful if you worked more on your own expression and reaction to that emotion? For example, if you realize that any time someone cries you get uncomfortable, try to change the subject, and physically leave the situation if they do not stop, then what can you do to develop more understanding of your own reaction. Where did the reaction come from? What meaning do you attach to crying? What can you do to reach a point where you can be in the presence of someone who cries and not lose your own empathic connection or effectiveness?

Working with strong emotion is one of the core essentials for good counselors.

BE ABLE TO LET PEOPLE MAKE THEIR OWN DECISIONS

Many people enter a counseling relationship confused and not able to make a decision of some kind—whether to get a divorce or not, whether to go to graduate school or not, whether to take chorus or orchestra, whether to tell their parents they are getting a failing grade in English or not, whether to get an abortion or not. Many decisions are even more confused and complex than the ones illustrated above—each of which was stated as an either–or kind of dilemma. Sometimes, clients want to make decisions and they are not even sure what the decision is about.

It is common for counselors to spend some time with clients and be able to see clearly what the situation is and what the simple answer is. It is very tempting at those moments to "just tell them what to do." Most counseling theories you will study would take a different approach than that; although, some counseling theories and practices are more inclined than others to actively give clients solutions to problems they presented.

To what extent can you let people make their own decisions? And, to what extent can you do that when the decision they might make is quite different than the one you would make in the same or similar circumstance?

I have known school counselors who not only would not encourage students to attend certain colleges, but who would actually discourage them from considering certain colleges because that college was a rival school to the one the school counselor attended. That is pretty extreme—but it happens. A counselor who entered college, tried engineering, failed at engineering, and became an artist might provide strong but subtle negative responses to a student who talked about engineering.

I once watched a counselor in training work with a young student. The student, a male, was expressing some interest in becoming an elementary schoolteacher. The counselor kept saying, "You wouldn't want to do that; men don't do that." The young student responded that he thought he would like it and, in fact, named a male elementary schoolteacher he knew. The counselor in training responded again, "But you wouldn't want to do that; what about…" (and she named a science and math-oriented occupation). Needless to say, the counseling student did not get a good grade on that exercise, but it did illustrate how the strong bias of a counselor (men should not be elementary teachers) worked its way into the counseling session. The student, when queried after the session, had no idea that she had been biased in her response. When questioned further, she acknowledged that she knew of no successful men in elementary education.

In some respects, to have a counselor watch a student make a decision they would not make himself or herself is a lot like parenting when parents, wanting their children to develop independence and self-confidence, watch their children make decisions the parents would not have them make. They know that there comes a time in the child's development when they will not be able to stand by and assure each decision the child makes, and they begin to pass that responsibility along incrementally as the child develops. Counselors do the same, so that the student who is academically talented and a high achiever who decides that he or she is not going to college presents a challenge to the school counselor who values higher education and knows that the student has great potential in several academic fields. This often presents a dilemma for counselors.

Just as with accepting strong emotion, counselors must know themselves well enough to know what their biases and strong values are and to know how those might interfere with the decision making of the clients they work with. It requires more self-examination.

BE POSITIVE AND OPTIMISTIC ABOUT POSSIBILITIES

It is important that counselors be able to see possibilities in otherwise difficult situations. This does not mean that the counselor should be extremely jubilant while standing in the midst of crisis, but it does mean that when clients or others get bogged down in life situations that seem impossible, the counselor must continue to envision positive outcomes or possibilities.

Positive optimism can be a real put-off for people who are depressed or caught in seemingly impossible situations. When clients are feeling down or trapped, they do not need to hear some sprightly quip about, "Cheer up, there's always a bright tomorrow!" What needs to happen is that the counselor in those situations can hear and understand the despair or the difficulty faced by the client, can reflect that back to the client so that the client knows he or she has been heard, and then help the client explore alternatives or help the client reframe some of his or her self statements so that the client can begin to see possible actions or alternate responses to his or her immediate dilemma.

It is difficult to be optimistic in the presence of despair. It is even more difficult, if you are the one in despair, to be confronted by overt optimism. The counselor's role in these situations requires a delicate approach.

It is probably important for you to examine the extent to which optimism is a core characteristic in your life. It does not need to be applied to a counseling situation—just examine what your typical reaction is to new events, challenges, evaluative situations, conflict, or any other condition. Do you go into a new activity saying to yourself that, "I won't be able to do this," or do you approach new situations with a positive outlook: "I can do this." When you have an exam at school, do you predict that you will not do well or do you anticipate a positive outcome? If you are to meet with a supervisor for a job performance evaluation, do you say in advance, "I'll probably get low marks in everything." When you meet new people, do you say to yourself, "They won't like me?"

Each of the illustrations in the paragraph above reflects the kind of internal message you might hear from a pessimist rather than an optimist. Of course, it is also probable that the internal messages quoted above are accurate statements based on other data you have. To take a positive view, however, would result in statements such as "I can do this," "I'm going to do well on this new activity," "My grade on the test will be a good one," or "My supervisor will see that I'm doing good work."

Overly positive or optimistic people may have as equally a distorted evaluation of self as overly pessimistic people. Good counselors would have accurate perceptions of themselves and of their clients with the ability to help clients look at their own self-perceptions and see possibilities that fit with accurate assessments. The counselor who meets with a student who has failed numerous classes, has poor attendance, has low test scores, and is enrolled in nonacademic subjects will have a difficult time if the student's overly optimistic self-statement is, "I plan to become a physician." The overly optimistic counselor meeting with the same student does not do a very good job if he or she says to the student, "Oh, wonderful, the world needs new physicians."

So what kind of person are you? Are you generally optimistic and see possibilities, or do you approach every event as if it will fail and you live just to be surprised? Your answer may suggest something about your personal qualifications to become a counselor.

BE ABLE TO WORK WITHOUT SPECIFIC REINFORCEMENT OR RECOGNITION

Success indicators for counselors are not as obvious as they are for persons who work with objects. A marriage counselor who works with a couple in conflict for five sessions has fewer indications of the success of his or her work than a brick mason who has a wall to build. The brick mason knows exactly when the wall is finished, and others can see the work and know if it is good or not. The wall will be there long into the future, and the brick mason can point to it years later and say, "I built that." The marriage counselor may see subtle changes in the way the couple relates to each other in the session, but there is less certainty about the success of the counseling sessions. The couple may stay together or not—and which of those actions is actually better in the long run?

If you are a person who must have a lot of feedback on the work you do in order to feel good about your work, then counseling may not be a good choice. The question for counselors is, "What do you need to be satisfied with what you do?"

There is a hazard for counselors who need a lot of feedback on their work—they may subtly (or directly) manipulate clients into telling them they are doing a good job. The counselor may not be overtly conscious he or she is doing this—it sometimes requires observations from an external observer or supervisor to help the counselor see that he or she is frequently making statements or asking questions that suggest the client should tell the counselor that he or she is doing a good job.

A parallel illustration might be made with young children in learning situations. Assume that there are two children of exactly the same ability: the young child who asks a teacher if he or she is correct after working on each math problem is different than the child who can do all the math problems and not have to ask for external affirmation of the child's accuracy.

The feedback to counselors about the quality and effectiveness of their work may be years in coming. It is sometimes immediate and direct—a client, who at the end of the session says, "I feel much better now and I can see a good solution," gives immediate feedback. The proof of the statement may require some time before its validity is known; and, in the meantime, the client may have reassessed what happened in the session and come to believe that it was not a good decision and that bad feelings remain. This just illustrates the complexity of the issues surrounding the question: What do you need to feel satisfied with what you do?

Satisfaction criteria can be examined in many situations. Potential counselors would do well to develop an understanding of their own requirements.

BE INTERESTED IN AND ABLE TO WORK WITH MANY DIFFERENT POPULATIONS

Some counseling positions will have a set of clients who are somewhat homogeneous. For example, a counselor working with entering college freshmen will be in contact with a large group, typically within a narrow age range and with a somewhat similar set of background skills. They might also be assumed to have some common goals—academic success in their initial college experience. Or, a counselor who has a job in a senior center working with clients who are experiencing their first placement in a residential treatment facility could be expected to find a number of similarities among the client group.

In most counseling situations, the client group for counselors will be much more diverse, and it is essential that counselors be able to work with many different populations. The differences counselors will encounter run the gamut of life experiences and life conditions—economics, health, race, gender, religion, values, behaviors—this is another list that could go on at length.

The question for persons intending to become counselors is to what extent are they comfortable and accepting of persons who are different than they are? And, to what extent do they have life experiences that let them develop some knowledge of persons who are different than they are?

Many educational institutions—from primary school through graduate education—will design experiences that give students a look at cultural experiences outside the normal zone of comfort for the students. Whether trips abroad to experience a different language and different culture or an experience in one's own community with people who may be different (e.g., working in a homeless shelter), the students who participate usually come back from those encounters with rich stories about what they learned through the exposure.

There are other methods to acquire information about populations different than one's own, including reading, media of several kinds, and classes, but my own preference is for persons to immerse themselves in cultural groups that will give them exposure and information about people who are different than they are. Like most of the other suggestions made in this book, it is important to be able to process the information or data that come from such experiences. The learner can do that in a variety of ways, but good discussion about what the different experiences mean and how they have an impact on one's own understanding of self and other is my own preferred method.

Special attention should be given to experiences that let you experience persons and cultures that differ by gender, race, culture, economic status, age, religion, and sexual orientation (this is not an inclusive list). If you are a white, middle-class Catholic, then attending a church in the African American protestant tradition will let you experience different things than usual. If you are a heterosexual, then reading material that informs you about the gay lifestyle is a start, and going with a homosexual friend to a gay bar or a protest demonstration will widen your vision. If you have always been in good health, then spending time volunteering in a hospital or clinic will let you see new things. You should design your own experiences, with suggestions from the persons who know you best and who can suggest what part of your life would profit most from expansion.

BE EMPATHETIC WITHOUT GETTING
"HOOKED" BY ANOTHER'S SITUATION

One of the most distinguishing characteristics of good counselors (and good counseling) is the ability of the counselor to empathize with the client. *Empathy* has been discussed in much of the counseling literature and, in some ways, is difficult to define. It often gets confused with *sympathy,* and people can generally explain what it is like to feel sympathy for someone or something. Empathy, on the other hand, refers to the ability to know and understand the feelings of another. Notice the two words used in the previous sentence to describe empathy—*know* and *understand*—both are cognitive terms, not affective or emotional terms. This illustrates part of the difficult and confusing line between empathic understanding and other feelings identified in emotionally charged situations.

Good counselors have the ability to feel with a client without having to feel what the client feels. Good counselors can express to the client words and phrases that communicate the level of empathic understanding the counselor possesses. Counselors should be able to communicate to a client that they understand the client's sadness without becoming sad themselves.

When people think about becoming counselors, some will say they could be good counselors because they have felt sad or depressed or angry or abandoned. Having experienced those feelings may be some help in understanding the feelings of others, but that is not the reason to become a counselor. Other people may think they should not be counselors because they feel along with their friends to the extent that whatever their friends are experiencing becomes what they are experiencing. That may indicate a level of interpersonal sensitivity, but it is not a good reason for becoming or not becoming a counselor.

A good counselor develops an empathic understanding of a client without getting so caught up in the emotion the client is experiencing that the counselor loses his or her own ability to function. This does not mean that a counselor is untouched by what he or she sees or hears from a client. It does mean that a good counselor has a strong enough sense of self that he or she can be present with another, understand and express to the other what his or her affect state is like, and yet not lose the counselor's self in the process—to not become enmeshed.

It is clear that counselors must have a good understanding of themselves and know how they react to strong emotion. In earlier chapters, there were several suggestions about how you might examine your own experience and reaction to strong emotion. I hope you discovered something about yourself and know how that characteristic fits with the potential to be a good counselor.

BE AWARE OF YOUR OWN BOUNDARIES AND BE ABLE TO MAINTAIN THEM

Just as good fences make good neighbors, good boundaries make good counselors. The word *boundary* seems simple enough, but it is a difficult concept to understand. And, when boundaries are violated or crossed, which frequently happens, counselors find themselves in trouble.

Charges of ethical violations by counselors very frequently are framed around the crossing of boundaries—a counselor and a client develop a romantic relationship, a counselor becomes personally involved in the life of a client and discovers that the professional relationship is no longer effective, or the client believes that the counselor has become a friend and begins to ask for things outside of the counseling relationship which enmesh the counselor. Each of these and many other illustrations are indicative of boundaries that have been crossed.

It is easy for boundaries to be crossed: a client asks for your home phone number so he or she can feel more confident in his or her ability to function without feelings of anxiety. Who would not be a nice person and give out something as simple as a phone number? And then the home phone starts ringing at all hours of the day and night—who would be such a terrible person that they would not answer it and provide the assistance that seems so simple to give? These are illustrations of how a boundary gets crossed and the situation begins to escalate quickly to a point where it is difficult to control.

Counselors can also initiate boundary crossing: Suppose that a counselor has a client who is, in all respects, a very likable person. The counselor sees in the client many characteristics he or she would admire in a friend—similar hobbies, similar interests, similar likes and dislikes in books and movies, and so on. Perhaps it is coincidental, but when the counselor encounters the client at a social event, it certainly would seem easy for the two people to interact as two good friends would interact. What is next? Generally, the next thing is a serious boundary violation—perhaps the party interaction was the first boundary crossing; or, perhaps the counselor's imagining the client as a friend rather than a client was really the first boundary violation. A boundary was crossed even before any action took place.

Professional counselors ascribe to a code of ethics that spells out in detail certain kinds of prohibited behaviors—boundaries. For example, a counselor must not have a romantic relationship with a client. It is the less well-defined boundaries that create difficulty for counselors and clients. Should you be a friend? When does a professional relationship end and a friendship begin?

Much of the personal value system found in good counselors calls on them to extend themselves to other people. Boundaries get crossed and professional relationships become compromised when those yearnings to be more of a helping friend than a professional counselor get in the way of effective helpfulness in the counseling relationship.

Boundaries will be something that counselors must pay attention to as long as they are in the counseling business.

BE ABLE TO TAKE CARE OF YOUR OWN PHYSICAL, EMOTIONAL, AND MENTAL WELL-BEING

Counseling is a demanding profession. To do a good job as a counselor, you must be at your best physically, mentally, and emotionally. It is essential to maintain good health as you continue to work as a counselor.

This does not mean that counselors are free of emotional problems or physical or mental issues. It does mean that counselors work on their own mental, physical, and emotional issues with appropriate therapeutic assistance just as you would expect a counselor to work through the issues related to high cholesterol with an appropriate physician or dietician.

Some people believe that a person should not become a counselor unless his or her life was somehow perfect—that they should not work with parents who have difficult children if their own children are difficult. On the other hand, some people believe that unless you have experienced exactly the same kind of situation or condition that a client brings to counseling that you could not possibly understand or work with a person in a counseling relationship. The logic of this belief falls apart if you consider how many life experiences or problems a person would have to have experienced in order to be a counselor with any kind of diverse client group.

The best thing that counselors can do is have a good understanding of their own issues and to assure that they are working on them with appropriate therapeutic assistance. This translates to mean that counselors need counselors. If that is hard for some people to accept, then they may not be the best candidates for the counseling profession.

BE INTELLECTUALLY CURIOUS AND
A CONTINUING LEARNER

Counseling is an intellectually demanding profession. Counselor education is equally demanding intellectually. The core knowledge base on which the counseling professions are built relies on concepts from psychology, sociology, anthropology, statistics, philosophy, and communication sciences. In addition, counselor education is almost exclusively a graduate-level preparation program; therefore, to even begin preparation for a counseling profession requires completion of undergraduate course work and degree with sufficient grade point average to warrant admission to graduate school in the institution of your choice.

The process of counseling demands focused attention of the counselor on what is being said and what is happening with the client or clients with whom they work. That means that the counselor must be cognitively and affectively alert to many dimensions of the client's words, meanings, feelings, and expressions—all the while maintaining a focus on self so that the counselor knows how personal reactions are occurring in order to judge that additional aspect of the counselor–client interchange.

Another way to describe the mental challenge of counseling is that the counselor must be totally aware of what is going on with the client, with himself or herself, and with the interaction between the two. This is like juggling several balls at the same time while taking care of numerous other factors, both mental and physical, and keeping track of all that has gone on before.

Counselor preparation requires a lot of reading—theoretical points of view as well as practical applications of theoretical positions. Counseling also demands a good bit of writing—during graduate school for numerous papers in classes and in practice to write or dictate case notes for each client.

Counselors frequently work with large amounts of complicated data in the form of test results, psychological reports, and related background studies. They may also be required to write similar reports in their role as counselors.

In an effort to always be on the cutting edge of both theory and practice, counselors need to regularly read new reports, journal articles, and books that explore new explanations of human conditions and situations. Counseling theory is in a continual state of flux, and counseling practice follows with changes based on the latest and best information available. Thus, counselors must always be in a learning mode.

Many counselors who have practiced their craft over several years will tell you that each year brings an increasing set of rules and regulations that apply to their counseling field. In particular, if the counselor works in a governmental or education agency, there will be an ongoing need to stay current on regulations that apply to the client group the counselor serves. In private practice, counselors are equally challenged to stay abreast of rules and regulations from insurance companies or other regulatory groups that affect their practice.

If you find mental challenges interesting and if you are curious about the things that make people the way they are, and if you see yourself as a helpful person who can listen well and not get so personally involved or enmeshed in what you are hearing that you lose perspective and objectivity, then counseling may be a viable career choice. Although a lengthy list to consider, the categories above are not comprehensive.

ADDITIONAL CHARACTERISTICS

I asked several experienced counselor educators what they would list as "essential characteristics" of good counselors. I received responses similar to the list I included at the beginning of this chapter; however, there were a number of characteristics I had not included or were described in an interesting way, which need to be listed and described here:

- Flexible
- Personable
- Genuine
- Assertive
- Energetic
- Consistent

Flexible

A rigid counselor will have a hard time personally and professionally. The practice of counseling requires a lot of adapting to ever-changing situations with clients. If a counselor insists on things happening a particular way, there will be a lot of frustration that results.

Flexibility is evident in other aspects of a counselor's practice. It is important for counselors to remember that clients are ultimately responsible for their own behavior and that the consequences of that behavior are theirs—not the counselors. Rigid counselors may frequently find themselves disappointed that clients do not take on the positive behaviors described as personal goals in the counseling session. Flexibility on the part of the counselor means that they can accept that outcomes are not guaranteed and that changes in therapeutic approach may be called for.

Personable

First impressions are important. When a client meets a counselor for the first time, it is important that the client's immediate initial impression be that of a person he or she can relate to. No one wants to face a counselor who looks grumpy, irritable, out of sorts, angry, cold, or distant. Counselors need to be personable.

Personable does not have to mean that the counselor is gushing with enthusiasm. They do need to project an attitude of caring for clients when they first meet as well as throughout the counseling sessions. I once knew a counselor who employed a rather manipulative device with counselees who did not seem to be working hard on addressing their issues: when the counselor felt the client was not working hard, he would pick up darts from his desk and toss them at a dartboard behind and to the left of the clients. The counselor would say, "When you're ready to get back to work, let me know." That hardly seems personable. On the other hand, the report is that clients often would dig deep into the issues that had brought them to the counselor in the first place—perhaps they would just do anything in order to stop the darts from coming so close.

Genuine

Clients may be among the best in the world in their ability to spot a phony. Counselors must be genuine. When they say that they care about a client, they should really care. Put-on attitudes and disingenuous comments are destructive of counseling relationships.

Counselors often convey attitudes toward clients through their nonverbal expressions. To tell a client to "go ahead and talk about that," and at the same time glance at a wristwatch tells a client in a strong message that he or she is not important—or, at least, what he or she has to say is not important. The body posture a counselor takes during a session tells a client a lot about the true feelings of the counselor. I used to have students watch videotape of counseling sessions with the sound turned off. There would often be a lot of agreement among observers about the attitudes being expressed by counselors through the way they leaned, nodded, or moved in a session. Once we made guesses about what the counselor was feeling, as expressed through nonverbal behaviors, we would rewind the videotape and play it with the sound on. That usually just reinforced the decisions we already made—even though at times the words being spoken seemed diametrically opposed to the attitude being expressed nonverbally.

Assertive

Being assertive is not the same as being aggressive—many people confuse the two. It is important for counselors to understand how to be assertive in those situations where action needs to be taken—as in a social justice situation—or individual rights are being compromised—either those of the counselor or the client. Being assertive is one way to define and reinforce healthy boundaries for counselors.

Counselors who work in agencies or educational settings may find themselves being asked to do things from time to time, which seem to benefit the institution more than they benefit the client. Those are times when counselors need to be assertive in defining the basis of what should be done and being able to speak up or act on those conditions.

Assertiveness may seem to some people to be uncharacteristic of counselors. If your picture of a counselor is someone who never disagrees, always "goes along," wants everything to be nice all the time, and only does what other people want them to do, this is not a picture of an assertive counselor. Being assertive does not have to mean being disagreeable. Because you are a counselor does not mean that you should be silent when someone tells a racist or sexist joke. An assertive counselor would find a way to call that person's attention to the fact that the joke is racist or sexist, explaining how it offended the hearer, and suggesting ways similar jokes could be avoided. Being assertive is a highly developed skill—it should fit nicely in the counselor's repertoire of techniques.

Energetic

Counseling takes energy. Some people might think that counseling is not a tiring process for counselors. Nothing could be further from the truth. Listening to people describe the difficulties in their lives and participating in the struggles they go through to find solutions can be both mentally and physically taxing.

Several years ago, a cartoon caught my eye—it showed two counselors leaving their offices at the end of the day. They were both dressed the same and were similar in appearance. As they closed their office doors, which were side by side in the hallway, one counselor, who appeared exhausted, disheveled, physically slumping, and obviously without energy, asked the other counselor, who appeared fresh, crisp, and full of energy, "How do you do it? How do you listen to all those people throughout the day and not get totally exhausted?" The second counselor, the fresh, energetic one, responded, "Who listens?"

The cartoon made its point. Counseling requires energy. This is another reason counselors need to be in good physical condition and to practice good self-care in physical and mental health.

Consistent

Counselors need to be consistent. Psychological experiments have shown that inconsistency in providing rewards and punishments for laboratory animals is one of the quickest ways to make them almost neurotic. If the behavior that results in a reward on one trial makes the animal get punished on a later trial, they do not know what to do. In parenting and in classrooms, children who get inconsistent messages—at first it is OK and later it is not—can easily slide into a pattern of behavioral problems. Both parents and teachers who are inconsistent in the messages they send to young people will discover that maintaining boundaries, discipline, and control become increasingly difficult.

Counselors who are inconsistent create the same dilemmas for clients. One of the powerful benefits the counselor provides a client is the presence of a known personage—an individual who will be the same from one session to the next. When the client's world is totally unpredictable, it is therapeutic to have a counselor who is predictable. This does not mean that the counselor is rigid—we already discussed flexibility above. Consistency and rigidity are not the same thing. Good counselors are consistent.

4

PREPARATION

If you decide that a counseling career is in your future, you need to do some serious planning about the preparation program you will need to complete in order to reach your goal. Depending on how early you start your planning process, there are several kinds of decision points ahead of you. In addition, depending on how specific you are with the counseling specialty you seek, there are other kinds of decision points ahead.

Let's start with the specificity question: If you decided on a counseling career that requires a particular license, it is essential to know what the licensing requirements are as you begin your educational preparation program. If you know that some kind of counseling career is in your future but you have not settled on a specific specialty, then it is important to build a broad-based educational program that will give you flexibility of choice as you move through it.

In general, counseling careers that do not require a license or certificate for entry are those entry-level positions for assistants, aides, staff workers, or beginning case workers. For example, the majority of staff positions for persons working in juvenile facilities may require a degree or a certain number of college credits but might not require that the degree be in a particular field. Similarly, persons who work in facilities that serve older persons or persons with disabilities might find position listings that require "an associate degree" or "2 years of college course work," but might not require that the degree be in a particular area. Those same kinds of positions might list job openings with the descriptor of a degree or course of study as a "preference," rather than a requirement, so that a person with a degree in psychology or sociology might be "preferred" in hiring but the particular degree might not be a requirement.

Counseling positions that require a particular license certainly fall into another category. If a position requires a license as a clinical social worker or a license as a school counselor, then the applicant must have completed a specific course of study and have passed the necessary licensing or certification requirements that accompany the title.

Because most counseling specialty preparation is at the graduate level, undergraduate course work becomes the first requirement in reaching your goal. Two things are primary in your considerations for a graduate school preparation program in counseling: (a) meeting the entry requirements for the graduate school you plan to attend, and (b) meeting the subject and content area requirements for the graduate program you plan to complete in order to reach the particular counseling career goal that you have in mind.

Entry to a graduate school usually requires two things in addition to an appropriate undergraduate degree: (a) sufficient grade point average to meet requirements, and (b) sufficient test scores (if required) on selected graduate school entrance procedures. To determine what these requirements are, you must study the graduate school catalogs for the particular degree program you have in mind.

Entry to a particular graduate program—for example, a specialization in social work, psychology, or counseling—may have additional requirements such as an experience record, interviews, or even an existing license in a related field. As an example, some school counseling preparation programs require that you have a license or experience as a teacher before entry. It is essential to read graduate catalogs carefully to make certain that you meet the requirements of the program you plan to enter.

How you make your choices about preparation programs depends on a variety of factors—how specific you are about the career goal you hold, how well you did in your undergraduate preparation program, what experience you have that you bring to the application process, where you wish to attend school, and what you can afford financially and with respect to time.

You can approach the requirement issues from one of two directions: You can begin with the college catalog and see what counseling career option would result from you going through a graduate program at a specific university, or you can go to the licensing requirements for a particular career option and work backwards, to see which graduate programs are most likely to lead to that license or certificate. The route you take may be determined by some of those other factors—finances, geography or school preference, or related issues.

Building an experience record to be an important part of your application can be done haphazardly or very intentionally. The haphazard way is to include whatever you have done for work or volunteer activity as part of your application (if experience is required) or it can be the result of careful planning on your part. If you know that you want to be a social worker with a specialization in mental health issues related to adjudicated juveniles, can you seek out a variety of volunteer and then paid activities that have logical connections to that specialization? These are the kinds of experiences that might begin in high school and continue through summer employment and paid or volunteer activity during undergraduate days. An admissions committee that can see that you have worked with youth in juvenile facilities is likely to look at you much more seriously than if your only paid- or volunteer-work experience is in a totally unrelated field.

Grade point average (GPA) in an undergraduate program is important in the application process for graduate school. Grade point average in particular course work that is related to the program emphasis may be even more important. For example, you might have an overall GPA that meets graduate school requirements for admission; however, if your GPA in counseling-related courses such as psychology or sociology is much lower than your course work in science and mathematics courses, an admission committee might be less inclined to view your application in a positive manner.

You may have loyalties to one academic institution and are not willing to even consider applying to any other school or university. Or, you may be limited geographically to one institution because of family obligations, finances, or other significant factors. That does not mean that you cannot pursue your desired career goal, but it might mean that you have to amend your plans somewhat. Suppose that you can only attend a local university and that you want to be a school counselor but the university only has a graduate program in mental health counseling and it is not possible to get a school counselor license with that degree. You may need to do additional planning to determine if there are additional institutions or additional course work that you can obtain elsewhere which, if added to the mental health counseling degree, would qualify you for a school counselor license.

The question of finances has to be examined. Graduate school is expensive, and like undergraduate education, is more expensive at private institutions and out-of-state universities, as a general rule. The expense of graduate school may be a little different than for undergraduate education based on your ability to be employed while you are going to school. Graduate education in one of the counseling professions usually requires a significant amount of practical work—practicum or internship courses—during the graduate program, and this work is frequently time consuming and without pay.

On the other hand, graduate education programs often have a variety of assistantships or fellowships for graduate students who are enrolled. As you are trying to decide which graduate institution to enter for your professional study, be sure to get all the information you can find about financial aid. It is a good idea to begin with the university's financial aid office, but you should extend your search to the program office for the degree specialization you will be working on. Frequently, degree programs have opportunities for the students who are enrolled, which will provide financial assistance through fellowships or research assistantships that are related to the area of study. As a general rule, that kind of information is best discovered through direct contact with the program officer who handles admissions. Another good place to secure that kind of information is with the department secretary. These people usually know whether there will be employment opportunities in the academic program area of your interest.

Examples of related assistantships you might find would be to work as a research assistant with a professor who has a grant to conduct a research project, or a graduate program in counseling might have a regular position with the athletic office to provide a counseling student with a certain number of hours each week where they work with athletes on academic and personal growth issues. If you have an undergraduate degree in certain areas, you might find that the university would have teaching assistantships in that area for you as you pursue your own study in the counseling area of your choice. There may be institutions in the community close to the university that regularly employ graduate students in counseling for the kinds of counseling-related functions that can be performed by persons even before they have received a final degree and license. An example of this kind of work would be working with youth in a residential treatment center or being a staff member in a correctional program or a case worker with senior citizens. You must take the initiative in finding the counseling-related positions in the community of your university. Of course, you will probably have good help in that through the admissions committee of the academic program you will enter.

All of the actions you take related to application and admission to a graduate program in the counseling specialty you have chosen must fit a time line defined by the university. Universities are well known for having published dates for receipt of certain materials, and it is common for materials received after those dates to be rejected, even though they might be of high quality. You can find the dates for required material in the catalog of the university you plan to enter. That kind of material will also be available on the university's Web page, and you should make and keep a copy of all the dates and deadlines and requirements that will apply to you as you go through a graduate program. The university will not hesitate to say, "Sorry, it's a day late so we can't accept it," and possibly thwart your best efforts at achieving some goal.

A concept that applies to university regulations that you should keep in mind is that the rules in place at the time you are admitted to a program are the rules that apply throughout your program. In other words, if the catalog in effect when you enter says that a certain degree requires 72 credit hours and a year later the requirement is increased to 75 credit hours, you can make a good case for sticking to the 72-hour requirement. The question the university will always ask is, "Under which catalog were you admitted?" As a student, you need to be assertive in looking out for your own interests in an academic program.

ASSESSING PREPARATION PROGRAM QUALITY

You will no doubt feel better about the school you select for your preparation program if you believe that it is a good school and that it will assist you in attaining the professional goal you have in mind. How can you tell if it is a good school or not? For this, you have to do a little digging.

Most colleges and universities go through a process of assessment and evaluation that results in program accreditation or program certification. When you read the descriptions of particular programs in a college catalog, you will often find that the school includes the names of different accrediting bodies for each of the programs or degrees it offers.

Make a list of the accreditations and certifications listed for the program you are interested in attending. Especially if you are entering a program that you hope will lead to you obtaining a particular license in one of the counseling specialties, you will need to check the list of accreditations against the licensing requirements for the state or states where you want to obtain a license in order to see if your school of interest meets the standards required of the licensing agency.

Licensing information can be obtained from the Web site for any state and for any specialty for which you have interest. I will explain more about that in a later chapter, but know that your starting point on checking quality is to see that if a license requires graduation from a program with a particular accreditation, that your school has that accreditation.

I believe that it is important to take your quality check even further. I suggest that you make a personal contact—phone, letter, or e-mail—with the licensing agency in the state you are interested in and ask a pointed question: "Do graduates from (name of university program) meet the requirements for licensing in (name the licensing specialty)?"

It is far better to discover in advance that graduates of a certain school do not meet minimum requirements for obtaining a specialty license than it is to learn that when you submit your application and get a painful rejection letter in reply. Some state licensing agencies may be able to give you additional data—number of applications from a university and the number of licenses granted. It is good to know.

A second kind of personal data searching you can do before applying for admission to a university program is to ask the program administrator for information about previous graduates: "What percentage of the graduates in the last 2 years have applied for and obtained licenses in (name the specialty of interest)?" You can also ask for employment data: "What percentage of your graduates who sought positions as counselors in (name the specialty) obtained those positions within the first year after completing their degree or course work?" These are the kind of questions a program administrator should be able to answer because it is incumbent on them to do the kind of follow-up studies of graduates that are required for various accreditation or reporting agencies. Do not be afraid to ask.

There are always explanations for the numbers of persons who are and are not employed following graduation. Employment percentages might drop when there are economic downturns and agencies put hiring freezes on the kind of positions you would seek. There are frequently people who enter licensing or certification preparation programs who do not intend to seek employment in that kind of professional position—they might be persons who love learning so much that they acquire degrees without the necessity of being employed in that same area. If this is the case in programs where the employment percentages are low, then program coordinators or others should be able to tell you that.

You are entitled to information about the outcome of education on the employment and other placement goals of graduates. Use the information to help you determine if the institution in which you are interested will actually help you reach your goals.

Use the checklist at the end of this section to help you work through some of the questions you might have about selecting a college or university and a graduate program that fits your chosen counseling specialty. And remember, one of the most valuable sources for information about a graduate program you might enter would be the students currently enrolled or the recent graduates with whom you might talk—and be sure to talk with more than one.

MY GRADUATE PROGRAM CHECKLIST

- I have a copy of the official catalog that would apply to my date of admission.
- The counseling career specialty I have chosen is included in the catalog.
- The program I would enter is accredited. The name of the accrediting body is _____.
- The degree I would earn will lead to a license or certificate in the counseling specialty of my interest.
- I checked with the state agency that licenses or certifies the counseling specialty I am interested in to verify that graduates of the program I am considering are eligible for licensing or certification.
- I obtained information from a program official or faculty member to determine:
  - The rate of successful completion of entrants _____%
  - The rate of successful licensing of graduates _____%
  - The rate of successful employment of graduates _____%
- I have information about employment opportunities and application procedures for graduate assistantships or research assistantships, and I talked with someone in the program about the possibility of obtaining an assistantship.
- I have information about financial aid for persons enrolled in the graduate program for the specialty I selected.
- I obtained information about what happens if I have to stop for a term or more because of health or personal issues, and I know what the procedure would be for resuming graduate studies in my field of interest.
- I have the names of at least three current or former students with whom I can talk and ask questions about the graduate program.
- I talked with at least one faculty member in the program to get answers to questions I have about the counseling specialty of my choice and program applicability.
- I have all the materials required for my application for admission, and I am aware of all dates and deadlines for the application process.
- I am pleased with the choice I made for graduate study in the counseling specialty of my choice.

II

This section presents a broad overview of the kinds of counseling positions found in a number of different settings. This is not a comprehensive list—a completely comprehensive list would be far too long to include in one book. I attempted to describe typical kinds of counseling positions found in five different settings.

Chapter 5, "Counseling in Educational Settings," provides sketches of the kinds of things counselors do at different educational settings based on the age of the pupils or students. The chapter also points out that what counselors do in one elementary school might be very different than what counselors would do in a different elementary school serving the same grades or the same-age students. Counselor functions are dependent on many things, chief among them being the supervisor—usually a school administrator—in the school. In addition, counselor–pupil ratios, socioeconomic conditions of the school, school district policies, and presence or absence of other social service specialists can have major impacts on the tasks performed by counselors in the school.

Descriptions of what counselors do are provided for preschool years, primary school years, elementary school years, middle school years, high school years, and college and university settings. Because there are so many different kinds of counselor roles in so many different school settings, the chapter concludes with suggestions about how you can learn more about counseling in schools. It also identifies the issues of licensing and certification again and concludes with a short list of some of the different kinds of counseling position titles found in various school settings.

Chapter 6, "Counseling in Private or Independent Practices," explains that there are a variety of kinds of counseling positions that can be found for private or independent practitioners. Some counselors work alone with no clerical or other help; others are members of large groups with specialized counseling functions distributed among the members. The kinds of colleague or partner relations that exist are also numerous. A good portion of this chapter explains the different ways counselors are paid for their services and emphasizes the need for understanding licensing requirements and the particular need for meeting insurance company regulations.

Chapter 7, "Coaching and Consulting," describes a variety of kinds of activities carried out by persons who identify as coaches or as consultants. The word *coach* is relatively new in the counseling and human service professions. Two persons who identify as a coach and a consultant are profiled in Chapter 13. Their experiences will inform the reader of this chapter about some of the advantages and disadvantages of working as either a coach or a consultant. Some people use both terms in addition to the title *counselor* in their work.

Chapter 8, "Counseling in Governmental and Agency Settings," introduces the reader to a wide variety of counseling positions to be found in city, county, state, and federal facilities. Several of the persons included in the profiles in Chapter 13 have worked or presently work as counselors in governmental settings. Governmental agency counselors are frequently salaried so that their income is not as dependent on the number of clients they see as it is for independent practitioners. Some counselors in governmental settings work with very narrowly defined client groups—for example, persons in addictions groups or juvenile offenders or clients in crisis situations. The chapter points out that employment in governmental settings or for public agencies is highly dependent on funding programs, and some counselors will find that if they have been funded by grant monies, employment ends when the grant funds end. There are satisfactions and stressors found among counselors in these agencies, just as in any other setting.

Chapter 9, "Counseling in Special Settings and With Special Populations," includes a number of different kinds of counseling positions as examples of the kind of work available in working with special populations. This is a wide-ranging descriptive term. It might apply to counselors who work in a center for victims of domestic violence, or it might apply to counselors who work with persons for whom English is not their first language. Special populations cover many different groups and settings. Persons seeking positions in these fields need to be creative about their job search processes.

This chapter also includes a discussion of how the electronic age has had an impact on counseling processes. It is becoming much more common to find counseling services offered by telephone or by interactive computer programs. There are a number of technical and ethical issues that arise in these situations, which professional associations and licensing agencies are continuing to resolve. For example, if licensing is a matter for each state and if a telephone counselor is in one state and the client in another, what regulations apply?

Readers should keep in mind that all the positions described in this section make up just a fraction of the different kinds of counseling positions that exist. And, there are new kinds of counseling positions emerging every day, just as there are new technologies emerging almost daily. I hope this section will give the reader a broad picture of possibilities.

5

COUNSELING IN EDUCATIONAL SETTINGS

Counselors work in many kinds of educational settings—from pre-kindergarten and early childhood education programs right on up through graduate and professional schools in colleges and universities. The things that counselors and other human service professionals do in the various education settings are as different as the settings are varied. (Note that the word *counselor* is used to describe many different position titles. A longer list of those titles can be found at the end of this chapter.) Job descriptions and job functions in an education setting are directed primarily by the guidelines and policies of the particular school and the supervisors or administrators for whom the counselors work more than they are by any standard or universally accepted position descriptions.

Counselors in education settings must be able to assess the particular individual and group needs of the students, teachers, families, and communities of the institutions in which they work. Understanding needs precedes development of individual and institutional goals and priorities. For example, secondary school counselors in a high school where there has been a long-standing tradition and a high family and community value on academic achievement and postsecondary education will have a different emphasis on their activities than counselors employed in schools where dropout rates are high and there is little value placed on college or university attendance. A counselor in a preschool that enrolls a high proportion of special needs children will have a different set of priorities and emphases than a counselor in a preschool that has a selective admission process based on potential in music and dance. A counselor in a middle school where there is a high level of gang violence and physical assaults will have a different job than a middle school counselor in a school with a 10-year history of peace and quiet among students and in the community.

So, when asked, "What do counselors in education settings do?" the answer is, "It depends." The one consistency for all counselors who work in any education setting is that the primary focus for their work is the student the school serves—whether that is a 3-year-old special needs child in a government-funded preschool, a bright 10-year-old in a talented and gifted elementary school, a troubled teen in an adjudicated-youth resident education program, a high school student who is struggling with family conflict, or a university junior who must declare an academic major.

In any education setting, counselors may spend some time doing any or all of the following activities: meeting with one student in a private office to listen to the student's concerns and assist the student in making decisions; meeting with a group of students, either in a classroom or in a separate group meeting room, to listen and help the students resolve some interpersonal or other issue; meeting with an individual teacher to discuss questions and concerns about a student or a group of students in a classroom; meeting with a group of teachers to discuss matters such as school climate or general student issues; meeting with a school administrator to discuss concerns about the school; or meeting with an individual parent or a group of parents to help them understand issues that one or more students are experiencing. This list could go on for many pages. In brief, counselors in schools work with individual students and with groups of students; they work with individual teachers and groups of teachers; they work with individual parents and groups of parents; and they work in consultation with administrators. In addition, counselors in schools might be actively involved with community groups that have student issues as part of their responsibility.

In general terms, the functions and responsibilities of counselors at different school levels could be described as follows.

PRESCHOOL YEARS

Counselors who work in schools with children before the age they would be enrolled in either kindergarten or first grade have a variety of job possibilities. The major issue determining the work of the counselor is the age of the child in whatever school setting the child is in. Preschool or preprimary or Head Start or Pre-K or day care settings all work with children before they are ready for school at either the kindergarten or first-grade level. Counselors in those settings spend a lot of time doing observations of children in their classrooms or play groups. Counselors might also spend time in the homes of children observing child–parent interactions or interactions between the child and siblings or playmates.

One of the counselor's objectives in doing as much observation as the counselor does is to make assessments of the child's development. The counselor might use the results of observations in the classroom, on the playground, or at home in making recommendations to teachers and parents about activities to help the child work through issues the child might have in behavior, social development, cognitive skills, nutrition, physical care, or any other characteristic observed in the various settings.

Counselors often work with other specialists in team meetings or staffing sessions to develop plans or individualized educational plans for a particular child. The counselor might use a set of observations across several children in the same preschool group to make recommendations to teachers about activities for a group of children, not just one child.

At times, counselors working in preschool settings may observe behaviors that lead them to believe that a child is being abused—physically, emotionally, or sexually. It is the counselor's responsibility in those instances to report his or her suspicions to the proper authorities who will conduct investigations to determine the validity of abuse suspicions or allegations. In nearly every state, laws have been passed that make it mandatory that counselors and other human service workers report their suspicions. Other laws have been passed that protect reporters from lawsuits brought by parents who have been unjustly accused. Counselors at every level must understand the reporting procedures and reporting regulations that apply in the school or setting in which they work and in the governmental unit that has responsibility for child welfare.

When the counselor in a preschool setting works with a child in a therapeutic mode, it often is through use of activity media, puppetry, art therapy, and structured tasks. (Counselors do not like to use the word *game* with therapeutic procedures.) Naturally, there is almost no "talk-therapy" used with preschool children. What the child says during some kind of story time or through use of puppets or drawing will be very revealing, and counselors must have a high degree of skill in order to be most therapeutically effective with children in those young years. The child probably tells the counselor more through activities, drawings, or movement than he or she does through words.

It is obvious that counselors in preschool settings must have an extensive knowledge of child development knowledge and must understand how the interactions of children with other children and with adults fall into different stages. Counselors must have a high degree of skill in being able to implement therapeutic practices through the efforts of other people—teachers, parents, classroom aides, and others.

PRIMARY SCHOOL YEARS

Counselors in primary schools will find that their jobs differ greatly depending on the number of pupils in the school or schools they serve and on the directives of the supervisors with whom they work. Small primary schools are seldom able to have a full-time counselor on staff; therefore, it is common for counselors to travel from school to school. Another model found in small schools is the counselor who has a split assignment—part-time counselor and part-time teacher.

The ratio of pupils to counselors is usually higher in primary and elementary schools than in secondary schools. Many counselors and counselor educators would argue against this trend and might say that ratios need to be lowest in the years with younger children; however, that is not the way most school systems assign staff.

Counselors in primary schools will do many of the same things described for counselors in preschool settings. One additional task common for primary school counselors is to conduct classroom activities that have a particular social or interpersonal focus at the core. For example, primary school counselors often go from classroom to classroom "teaching" students about friendship, safe touch, stranger danger, bullying, how to speak up and be assertive in threatening situations, and the like.

Counselors frequently will work with small groups of children who might have some issue in common. For example, a group of primary school girls whose parents are going through a divorce or a group of young boys who have difficulty on the playground. Being a group counselor with primary-age children requires a high degree of skill. It also requires a thorough knowledge of developmental psychology and of effective teaching or interactive skills. Counselors often are called on to conduct these sessions with a classroom, and one goal is to have the teachers in the classroom observe the counselor and the children during the activities in order to acquire new skills and new knowledge in the process. This allows the counselor to be viewed as a very skilled classroom instructor and not just a person who has escaped the classroom or who has avoided work with larger groups.

ELEMENTARY SCHOOL YEARS

Counselors in the elementary grades have similar functions to those working with primary school students. One of the differences that emerges in elementary or upper elementary grades is that the pupils, because of continuing maturation and development, begin to function more on their own or more independently. As a result, counselors in upper elementary schools may have occasion to work with students on a one-to-one basis as they address critical personal issues of childhood.

Counselors will continue to do numerous activities with groups of pupils. Many spend much of their time in classroom settings where they work with students and with teachers on activities to address social development, peer pressure, crisis issues, family relations, and the like.

At every school level, counselors will experience times when a crisis or some tragedy strikes and there is a need to work with individuals and students on issues related to death, illness, change, violence, abuse, or other issues. I remember vividly the first time that, as a school counselor, I had to inform a student that a parent had died. I also remember working with students in a school after the sudden death of one of their classmates. And I have vivid memories of my work in a school after a student brought guns to school and shot several people.

Some counselor activity in the elementary school is less likely to be in the open. Counselors at all levels will find themselves dealing with abused children, and they must know what their professional and legal responses should be in those situations.

It is relatively common for counselors in elementary schools to have a major responsibility with the testing program in the school. In some schools, the counselor will be the person who organizes and conducts all standardized testing. In other schools, the counselor may only be the person who uses test scores—either with individual students and their families or to explain aggregate results to teachers. At times, counselors will be called on to make presentations to parent groups about results of achievement tests or other demographic data collected from students.

Counselors will be participants, along with other staff members, in the development and implementation of individual educational plans. Counselors will be expected to contribute to the collection of data that go into the development of educational plans. They will also be expected to follow that portion of the plan that calls for particular therapeutic action or interventions conducted by the counselor.

MIDDLE SCHOOL YEARS

Whether your school is organized as a middle school, a junior high school, or some other administrative arrangement, counselors will have similar activities and needs in each. At an age when there are many tugs and pulls on the pupils in the middle school years, counselors can be busy all the time with the quickly changing issues of the day. The counselor's office can be filled with broken hearts one day and an eager group of budding scientists the next. Middle school years are years of rapid change.

Classroom teachers will continue to need consultation and assistance with individual student concerns around development, behavior, relationships, achievement, and parental conflict. The middle school years will find increases in individual acting-out behaviors on the part of students, many of whom will be experimenting with drugs or alcohol and many will be sexually active. The struggle for independence will take shape in many different forms, and middle school counselors often will find themselves helping parents understand the behavior of their child.

Middle school counselors will also have students who begin to explore options for their own futures. In a formal way, this will come when the middle school counselor works with students in making the transition to high school. Academic and career planning will become a larger part of the counselor's work.

The counselor will continue to be involved in standardized testing programs. And, the counselor will continue to function as a member of the pupil services team (or other name) that helps write individual educational plans for students who have been referred for evaluation or testing with subsequent placement in special programs.

HIGH SCHOOL YEARS

Counselors in schools with high school students can expect to be involved with many of the struggles of adolescents, which are played out between students and their parents, with teachers, and within peer groups. High school students, in their struggles for independence and self-identity, test the limits of many adults. A good counselor is required to be able to establish good relationships with them and to assist them through the many trials and tribulations that come their way.

High school counselors will be involved in helping some students plan for their futures—career choice and postsecondary school plans. Counselors will be working with other students on crises of the moment—whether to stay in school or drop out. The social stresses of adolescence seem to increase with the age of the student, and counselors will find that it takes a lot of skill to work in one-on-one sessions or in group sessions with students and the kind of struggles and choices they have.

The therapeutic role of counselors is limited in some schools. Counselors can meet with students about academic planning or career choice for a fixed number of sessions individually—perhaps three sessions in a year. If counselors sense a need to meet more than that number, they are encouraged to refer the student to other human service workers—either in the school or in other social service agencies. In this kind of setting, the picture of the high school counselor as involved in therapeutic interventions is certainly limited.

In other schools, counselors might have a major portion of their role be involved in counseling sessions with individual students. The format for delivery of service varies widely.

In some schools, counselors might be heavily involved in school and classroom attendance. In others, attendance matters may be the domain of other staff members and counselors can focus on academic advising, career choice, and classroom interactions. Counselors will be expected to be resource persons for administration and interpretation of standardized tests. They will also have a customary role in helping students make the transition to school—whether as new students in the community or as new classes move to the high school from junior high school.

Counselors in senior high schools, perhaps more than those in elementary or junior high school, are frequently viewed by classroom teachers as part of the administrative structure of the school. Whether they actually are classified as administrators, teachers, or some other label will depend on the official organization of the school and whether there is a union contract or negotiated agreement that specifies who represents counselors in salary negotiation, collective bargaining, or other contractual relations.

If counselors are perceptually viewed as administration by classroom teachers, it can set up a different kind and level of expectation in the communication between the two. If counselors are officially classified as teachers, that also changes the kind of relationship they have with classroom teachers and other staff. A good question to ask counselors in informational interviews is how they are classified and how they are perceived by classroom teachers—as colleagues or as members of management or administration? A follow-on question is to ask how that perception affects the way they work with others in the school building.

A critical question that is growing in intensity is the issue of whether people see themselves as school counselors or as counselors in schools.

In some school districts, there is a growing trend to have school counselors do less work with students on an individual basis and more in classroom groups. Other persons (counselors in schools) might be assigned to take up the responsibilities of working with students on a one-on-one basis or on more therapeutically critical issues. The two positions will no doubt continue to receive a significant amount of attention in the professional literature.

COUNSELORS IN COLLEGE AND UNIVERSITY SETTINGS

Many different kinds of counselors are found in college and university settings. On the one hand, universities usually have counseling centers established on campuses that are staffed by licensed doctoral-level counselors and psychologists. In some instances, when students make appointments in a college counseling center to see one of the therapists, it is like going to an independent practitioner who bills the student's insurance company for providing service. Other universities may provide unlimited therapeutic service to students with costs covered by general student fees. In the same facility, other kinds of counselors may be housed who are not licensed as psychologists or counselors but who work with students on specific issues defined by student status or condition.

In general, counseling services in colleges and universities fall under an organizational label such as "student services" or some other inclusive term. There may be many persons who work in admissions, orientation, tutoring, academic advising, and career counseling who have some counseling preparation but many who do not. The positions usually associated with the categories just named do not require any kind of license or certification for the person to do the work involved. Universities will place their own requirements on persons hired for the work, but for rare exceptions, the only positions requiring licensed counselors would be those in university counseling centers. Even there, universities have a lot of flexibility about the certification and licensing requirements for persons they hire.

Academic departments—engineering, music, liberal arts, and so forth—may employ persons to function as advisors—they may even be called counselors. They may advertise the positions in a way that says they "prefer" persons with a degree or course work in the same academic major in which they will be advising, but it is probably not a requirement. For those permanent or full-time academic advising positions on a college or university campus, persons generally need to have completed an undergraduate degree to meet the entry requirements. Whether the person needs a graduate degree may depend on whether the position (such as academic advisor) is identified as a faculty position or as a classified position without faculty status or rank.

The level of preparation required for academic advising positions on a college campus may also depend on how significant are the decisions the employees make as part of their work. A college might be willing to employ students in part-time positions to give orientation tours to new or prospective students, but they probably want a full-time employee with university-determined credentials to be the one who signs off on enrollment decisions that obligate the university to a particular set of courses that make up a degree program.

Career counseling centers are frequently found on college and university campuses. On some campuses, they are divisions or components of the campus counseling center. On other campuses, they may be free-standing service programs. On still others, they may be service programs offered by an academic program such as counselor education, where graduate students in counseling regularly provide career counseling services under supervision as part of their graduate preparation program. Other campuses, particularly large, complex universities, may have career or academic counseling programs organized and operated within each academic or degree-granting unit in the school. There are many models available.

Counselors are often found in special programs on college and university campuses. For example, athletic programs frequently employ full-time or part-time counselors to work with athletes. Depending on the size of the athletic program, there may be counselors for different sports within a university athletic system—one counselor who works with women's gymnastics and another who works with basketball players, and so forth. The responsibilities of counselors in those kinds of programs are always interesting to consider in terms of potential ethical conflicts—is the counselor primarily concerned about the individual athlete or is the counselor essentially focused on the success of the particular sport where they are employed? In the first case, a counselor might be working with an outstanding athlete who is leaning toward dropping out of the sport in order to pursue other interests. The counselor might listen, reflect, help clarify, and explore resources with the athlete and accept the final decision—whether it is to stay or go. In the other situation, the counselor might be inclined to influence the athlete to remain on the team, at least until the season is over and the sport has gained success. For counselors in those settings, the question always is, "Who is my client—the athlete or the sport?"

Other counselors might work with special populations of college students—first-generation college attendees, international students, sexual-minority students, women, ethnic-minority students, older-than-average students, students on academic probation, returning students, veterans, or any other population large enough and with special needs identified with which skillful counselors can assist.

A question that always arises with counselors in special population programs is, "Must you be a member of the special population in order to be a good counselor with the special population?" In other words, must you be female to work as a counselor in the women's program, a sexual minority in order to work with sexual-minority students, a first-generation college student to work with first-generation students? Graduate students in counseling programs will no doubt have that debate at some point in their academic program.

An intriguing issue for counselors who work in college and university settings relates to matters of individuality and privacy. Older counselors can remember a time when parents had access to nearly all the information related to their college students. Persons who work with college students must be informed about laws and regulations covering personal information. Changes in legislation concerning family rights and privacy have shifted the issues of who controls personal information for college students and generally puts all information control in the hands of the student. There is no longer a letter that goes home to the parents from the college informing them that their student's grades are slipping or that their student has been seeing a counselor for matters related to depression. This kind of situation comes rushing into the public eye after events on campuses where it is discovered that preliminary signs of serious mental health disturbance were known about a student but that parents and others were not informed in advance. Counseling students in graduate school usually spend a good bit of time studying legal precedent on matters of collection, maintenance, release, and disposal of student records—whether they are records of attendance and grades in a course or records of visits to a college counseling center. When these matters hit the public media, it nearly always sparks heated arguments on limits of privacy and confidentiality for college students.

Colleges and universities provide a wide variety of work opportunities for counselors. If this setting is one that interests you, then you should begin your search early to discover one of the several jobs that may be available in the future. Good wishes.

HOW DO YOU LEARN MORE?

You should talk with counselors who work in education settings and ask them about the things they do; you will find that the list is different for counselors in different schools. If you are interested in a career in an education setting, you would be well advised to collect position descriptions from several institutions for the levels at which you think you might like to work. Use what you learn from the different position descriptions when you have a personal interview with a counselor who works in an education setting. Informational searches and informational interviews should not be limited to one school or one counselor. Two counselors who work in the same school might have different job responsibilities or might approach their work very differently. If you talk with only one person, that person's position might be unique and not something you would like to do at all. In a similar fashion, a single position description could be very atypical of the same title for other education institutions—even those in the same district and at the same level. Be thorough in your search.

On a humorous note, when asked about the responsibilities listed in their position descriptions, most counselors in an education setting will toss out the phrase "ODAA." This stands for "other duties as assigned." It is found as a part of many formal position descriptions—often the last item in a list of duties—and is used to cover a multitude of assignments, some which the counselor might have said "no" to if they had been spelled out in advance of taking a job. ODAA may also constitute a set of tasks that have no known connection to a good counseling program but have been added to a counselor's job by a supervisor or administrator. In an informational interview, you should ask counselors what is included in the ODAA category and how much time they invest in those functions.

A third source of information about what counselors do in different education settings is to examine descriptions of ideal positions as described in textbooks. A fourth source is to read statements from professional associations about the ideal role of counselors in education settings. Organizations such as the American School Counselor Association, the National Association of School Psychologists, and the National Association of School Social Workers have published position papers that describe appropriate roles and functions of counselors in schools. At the university level, the American College Personnel Association, the American College Counseling Association, the National Association of Student Affairs Administration, and the National Student Personnel Association have statements describing appropriate role and function.

Because school administrators often are the direct supervisors of school counselors, it is a good idea to study what is included in the role and function of administrators as defined by professional association statements. For example, the National Association of Secondary School Principals (NASSP) has articles on counselors' roles in their literature, much of which can be found on the NASSP Web site.

LICENSES AND CERTIFICATES

States control public education; therefore, regulations about who can work in public schools (and private schools) are controlled by state regulatory organizations. In order to find out what licenses or certificates are required to work in a counseling position, it is important to search through the state's licensing and certification regulations. Most states will have this information available on Web sites devoted to education. If you discover, for example, that school counselors must have a state teaching certificate or license as well as a state counseling certificate or license in order to be employed in a public school, you should determine if you can meet those requirements. If not, what education, training, or experience do you lack in order to meet minimum qualifications? When you determine the specific certificate or license you desire, will the preparation program you are considering actually provide you with all the necessary course work and competencies? You should remember that requirements and the names may differ from one state to the next; therefore, if you plan to work in a state other than the one where you receive your education, it is important early on to check the regulations in the state (or states) where you anticipate employment. Make your intentions clear to advisors in your preparation program.

There are numerous questions you need to answer before you can feel confident about the path to your employment goal. Do not hesitate to ask specific questions along the way:

- Have you decided what level of education or what age group of students you want to work with?
- Have you decided in what states you are most likely to seek employment?
- Can you select two or three education settings that are similar to your intended work setting?
- Have you obtained descriptions of what counseling professionals do in the education settings of your interest?
- Have you obtained position descriptions for counseling professionals in the education settings of your interest?
- Have you scheduled an interview with a counseling professional in two or more education settings?

- Can you get approval to shadow a counseling professional in one or more of the education settings representing your interest?
- Have you discussed your findings and your experience with colleagues or instructors to determine how well the positions fit your own strengths, characteristics, skills, and intentions?

Some positions in education settings may not require licenses or certificates. People may be employed or volunteer in education settings in human services positions without state-level certification or license when the education institution has created special programs or special jobs. For example, it is common for high schools to organize in-school centers or programs for college and career searchers, which are staffed by volunteers. These volunteers, or part-time employees, usually have completed a focused training program and are usually supervised by a certified teacher or counselor. Classroom aides are employed in a wide variety of positions. The similarity in each of these situations is that at some point, they are officially supervised by a certified or licensed person, even though they may practice some of the skills and perform some duties of the certified employee. These situations are nearly always school-specific, and you cannot assume that a position you would enjoy in one school exists in any other setting. Information about this kind of situation can be obtained from a school district's human resources or personnel department:

- Have you found the certification or license requirement(s) for the counseling positions you are interested in?
- Have you found the certification or licensing agency in the state or states where you think you might want to be employed? (Use your Web browser to search for "position title" + "state name" + "certification" and "license.")
- Have you determined if the preparation program you are in or are considering entering provides the essential education and experience supervision to meet minimum certification or licensing requirements?
- Have you talked with a faculty advisor to assure that your preparation program will meet requirements for certification or licensing?
- Can you verify through university catalog requirements that the certification or licensing program you are interested in is included in your plan of study?
- Do you know the application time line and application process for the certification or license of interest?

POSITION TITLES

A few of the position titles found in education settings that relate to the counseling and human services field are as follows:

Counselor
School Counselor
Social Worker
School Social Worker
School Psychologist
Mental Health Counselor
Advisor
Academic Advisor
Dean of Students
Behavioral Specialist
Instructional Assistant
Career Counselor
Guidance Counselor
Child Specialist
Child Development Specialist
College Counselor

6

COUNSELING IN PRIVATE OR
INDEPENDENT PRACTICES

Many people hold an image of a counselor or therapist as a person in a nicely appointed private office with a receptionist in an adjoining waiting room. In their idealized picture, the therapist sees six to eight clients a day, each one for a 50- or 55-minute session. This image is often reinforced by what people see in movies, television programs, or other media presentations. For many, the idealized image becomes their occupational goal without realizing that there is much more to the picture of a counselor or therapist in private or independent practice than the brief picture described above. In addition to the visible portion of a private practitioner's work, there is much more that neither the client nor the public ever see. For some, the discrepancy between the initial expectation and the final reality of a profession in an independent practice may be so great that they leave the field. Others find ways to make a professional position in an independent practice a satisfying career.

A few therapists fit the picture painted in the opening sentences above; however, many pieces are missing from the picture presented in the idealized setting. I will try to sketch in some of the critical elements for independent practitioners. The title of this chapter uses both *independent practice* and *private practice*. *Independent* practice is a broader term than *private* practice—both will be discussed in this chapter.

There are many different configurations of private practice. On the one hand, there is the sole practitioner—one person who does it all, including clerical work, accounting, therapeutic work, and janitorial cleanup. On the other end of the spectrum is a clinician who is a member of a large group of therapists joined together in some kind of professional and business organization who has numerous staff persons ready to provide all the support services the clinician requires but does not directly provide. In between are a variety of other configurations that all fall under the rubric of private or independent practice.

Independent practitioners can be organized as individuals who merely have adjacent offices and a shared receptionist, or they might all be partners organized as a legally binding group where the positive and negative actions (liabilities) of each partner and the income generated are distributed among all members. The more common procedure is to have income distributed based on how much each practitioner generates from seeing clients.

To understand the scope of what private practitioners or independent practitioners do, take a look at the Yellow Pages of your local phone book. Check the categories of *counselor, therapist, psychologist, marriage and family therapist, family therapist, social worker,* or any other human service occupational title common to your area. Look at the advertisements and see the kind of services provided by persons in each of the listings. When you look at the names of professionals listed, you may see some who are part of a group and others who do not appear to be connected to any other practitioner. The list or number of different specialties or conditions they include in their advertisements may appear overwhelming.

If you pursue informational interviews with independent practitioners, and I strongly encourage you to do so, talk with someone who is truly a sole practitioner, not working with or in partnership with any other professional. Try also to interview one or more persons who are part of a group that practices together. It is important in making a decision about your future that you see the full range of work settings under the category of *independent practice.*

LICENSING, EDUCATION, AND CERTIFICATION

Licensing

There are many paths on the trail to become an independent practitioner. Because states control or regulate the practice of independent practitioners, it is important to include in your own search an exploration of the rules and regulations that would cover you in the state where you intend to practice. Usually, these rules can be found with Web searches using combinations of key words—the name of the state and the word or words *license, certification, counselor, psychologist, social worker,* or *marriage and family therapist.* For example, if you Google "Oregon licensed counselor," you will be taken directly to the state board that licenses counselors with a full range of questions and answers (frequently asked questions, FAQs) about requirements and processes. Another example would be "Oklahoma licensed psychologist." You will find a link to the Oklahoma board that examines and licenses psychologists. Do the same for the states that interest you and see what differences you find. There may be other words you wish to include in a Web search of regulatory bodies—perhaps you have a particular kind of practice in mind. Use the search words that describe your own interests or ideas, and find the state regulations that cover that particular practice. For example, if you were interested in knowing about the requirements to be a counselor for persons with gambling addictions in the state of Illinois, a Web search (Google) on "Illinois gambling addiction counselor license" will take you to several hot links. Included will be the requirements to become an addictions counselor in several different states, including Illinois.

Sometimes, state Web sites that cover licensing or certification requirements may not be easy to read. It may be helpful to have those regulations or guidelines in hand when you do informational interviews with practitioners. Have them help you understand what a person needs to do in order to be qualified for the specialty of interest.

Education

Just as it is important to understand licensing or certification requirements for an occupational title that you see as your goal, it is also important to be certain that the educational program you would enter can provide the required preparation for you to reach your goal. If you understand the licensing or certification requirements for a particular profession, use those to test the educational program for compatibility. Read the college or university catalog carefully about claims that a training or degree program will let you attain your goal. A university preparation program cannot guarantee that you will be licensed—only that you will be able to take the course work required for a license or certificate. The rest is up to you—to pass licensing or certification exams and to meet the other requirements set out by the state.

When you apply to an education program, ask specifically if the course work you intend to take will meet your goals. Ask for copies of university handbooks or catalogs that confirm that information and make certain that you retain copies of those materials as of the date you enter the program. In nearly all institutions of higher education, the catalog that is current at the time you enroll will be the set of rules that apply to you, even if the rules change before you graduate. Keep your own dated copy.

A good question to ask when you are choosing a school is whether the degree program you want to enter results in a person being fully eligible for licensing or if there are postgraduate requirements students must complete at their own expense before meeting full eligibility. Everything you need to obtain a license or certificate might not be included in a graduate program, even in a comprehensive and high-quality graduate program. For example, some practitioner categories require a certain number of clock hours of clinical practice under supervision before a person can obtain a license or certificate. Those hours might or might not be included in the graduate program you are considering.

Certification

Throughout this chapter, I used the words *license* and *certificate*. There are differences between the two, and there are differences from state to state. The generally accepted definition, however, would use the word *license* to indicate a credential that means you are entitled to call yourself by a particular title, such as *psychologist* or *licensed clinical social worker* or *licensed marriage and family therapist*. In states that have licensing laws that cover these practitioners, a person must have completed all the requirements required by the state licensing body before he or she can use the particular title of that license. Other states may have certification laws. A certificate usually indicates that you completed some kind of special training, but it does not necessarily have to be training from a graduate school or university. In some states, it might be possible to call yourself a *counselor* or a *therapist* without having a certificate or license. In other words, state laws might not prohibit the use of the title, but they might also have a body that certifies persons as having met educational and experience requirements in order to be a "certified" counselor or therapist of some kind.

A second kind of permission or prohibition associated with a license in many states is that only license holders (in some states) are legally permitted to do certain kinds of clinical processes. As a typical example, some states might say that only a licensed psychologist can perform psychological evaluations on which disability payments might be based. Or, in most states, you cannot use the title *psychologist* unless you hold that license; whereas, you might not be prohibited from calling yourself a *counselor,* even if you do not have a counselor license or certificate.

Know what the state where you intend to practice requires. You can also see these differences by studying the Yellow Pages of your phone book. Which practitioners identify themselves as *licensed* and which as *certified*? When you do your informational interviews, ask about the differences as the person you are interviewing sees them.

COUNSELOR INCOME

Licensing or certification may also be a critical factor in how practitioners are paid. Health insurance companies and health maintenance organizations will have explicit requirements to identify the practitioners eligible for reimbursement for services rendered. When you talk with different practitioners, ask how they work out the relationships with insurance providers. Many will probably complain about the amount of paperwork required to submit claims for payment, the provisions and restrictions on who can be paid and for what, and the delay between providing service and receiving reimbursement. Others may identify qualification for insurance company reimbursement as a comfortable guarantee of an income stream. It is a common topic of discussion among independent practitioners and one to be thoroughly examined in an informational interview.

Insurance Payment

The health care industry and health insurance have undergone tremendous changes in recent years. Health care is a hot topic among politicians in any election, and the rising cost of health care is usually an item discussed early in the negotiations for labor contracts and other matters of employee compensation. Insurance companies usually limit who they are willing to pay for services, and mental health services are a prime example of how changes in who can be a service provider have had a major effect on the mental health business—private practitioners being right in the center of that conflict.

Employees in a large company who have several insurance companies available to them may discover that one company pays for some mental health services and another company does not or it may pay for a different number of sessions for the same condition. For the private practitioner, this dilemma comes to the foreground when he or she has a client with whom the practitioner could work, but the client may be covered by a company that does not pay for the kind of service needed. Or, the company may pay for service provided by one kind of licensed professional but not another—for example, the company may pay for marriage counseling provided by a licensed clinical social worker (LCSW) but not by a licensed professional counselor (LPC). Some counselors have engaged in unethical behaviors in these situations in order to receive payment. They may treat a client for one condition that is not reimbursable by an insurance company but might submit claims for payment by labeling the client's condition with a diagnostic category that is eligible for reimbursement. This practice puts both the client and the counselor in a very untenable situation.

Private practitioners have the task of demonstrating to insurance providers that they meet the requirements demanded of the company in order to be "an approved provider." In addition, once a practitioner is recognized as an approved provider, the practitioner must follow the guidelines of the insurance company in submitting required forms for payment of services. For the person who practices alone, managing the paperwork that goes along with reimbursement for service paid by insurance companies can be a daunting task. Some practitioners have decided to forego insurance payments as a source of income because of the hassle. For practitioners who are part of a group large enough to have a person or department responsible for billing, the hassle is somewhat relieved.

Personal Payment

Some private practitioners are paid for their services directly by the clients they serve. In one respect, they have the least amount of hassle in their professional lives over payment—the client who receives service writes a check to the practitioner. Of course, the counselor must still establish fees for service, decide if a client is billed the full amount per session or if the client receives services for a reduced rate, and have some form of collection for the counseling service—either a billing system or cash on demand at the time of a session.

The advantage of working just for personal payment is that the counselor is free to set fees and has total discretion about flexibility in those fees. The major disadvantage is that clients need to be persons who can afford to pay for counseling service. Working on a personal payment option means that the counselor must decide about the amount of time or service he or she will provide on a pro-bono basis for clients unable to pay. Counselors, as a group, care for people. There are personal and professional conflicts that can arise when the client is paying for services out of pocket and the counselor knows that funds are limited—perhaps to the extent that the client is making choices between getting counseling or purchasing family necessities. To what extent should client hardship have an impact on the kind or amount of counseling one receives? Hopefully counselors do not have to struggle with this question often.

Governmental Support

Some counselors work for governmental agencies and are paid a salary, so that their income is not dependent directly on the number of clients they see. Other counselors who have contracts for service to governmental agencies know that they will be paid a certain contracted amount for each client they see. These counselors usually are not required to bill clients or to collect fees from individuals. Their system of payment might require that they submit records or reports to an agency indicating which clients they have worked with, or they might be asked to indicate the number of client hours provided in a specific time period, but because services are paid for by the agency, there is no direct negotiation with clients about payment.

A related kind of counselor relationship with governmental agencies could reflect a shared payment procedure. The counselor might have a contract with a state, county, or city government to provide services to a client group on a sliding scale based on the ability of the client to pay. These systems usually require the counselor or someone in the counseling agency to interview a potential client about ability to pay, and a fee share is negotiated with the client paying some of the counselor's session fee and the sponsoring agency or governmental unit paying the rest.

Counselors who depend on contractual arrangements with governmental agencies for income based on fees for service to defined clients must always be concerned about the length of time for the contracts and the vagaries of change in governmental funding. In economic hard times, governments look for ways to cut costs, and the human services often are targeted. A counseling group might have a 3-year contract to provide counseling services to juveniles who are connected to the court system. At the end of the 3-year period, will the contract be renewed or not? Depending on how much of the counseling group's total revenue is tied to the one contract, nonrenewal could mean a precipitous change in revenue in a relatively short time. Counselors in this kind of group must devote a significant amount of their noncounseling time to developing new contracts and maintaining old ones in order to have a predictable income stream.

Employed Counselors

Some counselors are employed by businesses, companies, or governmental agencies on a retainer or other fee structure to provide services to persons connected with those organizations. Counselors might be on a system where they are paid an amount each month independent of how many hours of service they provide. Others might be paid a flat rate per month as retainer with increases in payment if the number of service hours exceeds some established minimum. These counselors are very much like private practitioners or independent contractors, but they know that their client group comes primarily from the employing agency or business. For example, a private practitioner might have a contract with a city to provide counseling services to police officers and firefighters who experience stress on their jobs. The counselor can be considered "on call" and might go for long periods without requests for counseling; then, there might be a tragedy in the community and firefighters and police officers could be lining up for counseling service.

I have a friend who is a family therapist who had a continuing retainer with a banking group. At any time there was an armed bank robbery, he might be called to rush to the scene and work with the employees who often experienced severe emotional trauma—frequently trauma that would not show up for some days or weeks after the actual robbery and that might be triggered by seemingly unrelated events. The therapist's work was based on the frequency of bank robberies in his area.

There is a certain amount of income stability in the kind of arrangement described above; at the same time, unpredictability is obvious. The format might vary a great deal from company to company, but the combination of guaranteed income plus additional income when service hours go over the minimum provides a degree of security and flexibility for the counselor. The negotiations about what to charge for service are done at the time of the original hire or the original contract rather than with each client as he or she meets with a counselor.

SO WHAT DO INDEPENDENT PRACTITIONERS DO?

To answer the question "What do private practitioners do?" more than a cursory glance is required. The opening sentence of this chapter referred to the idealized image that many people have of private practice. That image comes from a variety of sources, including the many portrayals of private practitioners presented by the media, a person's personal experience having been in one or more counseling sessions, knowing a private practitioner, study, or any one or a combination of other information sources available to people. To really get to know what private practitioners do requires more digging.

One difficulty about the common image of private practitioners is that the media have had a heavy influence on what we think counselors do. I suggest that you make a list of all the counselors, psychiatrists, psychologists, social workers, and other therapists whom you can identify from movies, television shows and news stories, novels, newspaper, or any other media format. Your list might include the psychologist played by Bob Newhart in a long-running television series *The Bob Newhart Show,* the therapists played by Judd Hirsch and by Robin Williams in the movies *Ordinary People* and *Good Will Hunting.* You might picture the therapist who works with Monk on the television series *Monk,* or you could envision the therapists played by Barbra Streisand in *Prince of Tides* or Billy Crystal in *Analyze This.* Two television series—*Friday Night Lights* and *The Sopranos*—have a school counselor and a psychiatrist as main characters. Each of these private practitioners is flawed in some way, and professional counselors or counselor educators might wince when they watch the films; however, many viewers may walk away from the show thinking, "That's what I want to be."

To get the best picture of private practice, you probably need to carefully interview several practitioners. To get a sense of what private practitioners do, begin with the telephone book listings: Check the Yellow Pages and see what other listings of practitioners you have in your community. Examine what they say they do in the classified advertisements. What titles do they use, what licenses do they list, and what specialties do they include among the things that describe who they are?

If the practitioner lists particular licenses or certificates, go to the Web sites of those licensing agencies and see if there is a list of duties that persons with that license can and cannot do. When a practitioner lists certification of a particular specialty, check out the description of that specialty on the Web and in other materials you can find to see what the specialty certification means.

Once you have prepared yourself with as much information as possible about the functions of private practitioners, select two or three who fit what you think you might want to be and see if you can schedule an appointment for the purpose of learning more. Be clear about your purpose—you are not coming as a new client; you are an inquiring person who is considering your own professional future, and you want to learn as much as you can from the practitioner. Most private practitioners will grant you a block of time to help you in your career decision process.

You may find there is a wide range of settings in which private practitioners work. Offices may be neat, austere, spare in their furnishings, or you may find large, elaborate, artistically decorated surroundings. What does the setting and appearance say to you about the person you might be interviewing? What would it say to you if you were a new client coming into the room? Are diplomas and licenses hanging on the wall? If so, what do they say to you as a visitor or as a client? Does the artwork on the walls or do the books on the bookshelf tell you anything about the philosophy or orientation of the counselor? For example, do the books or pictures tell you that this is a safe place to mention anything about sexual orientation? Or, is everything in the office so neutral that you can take no meaning from the visual aspect of the office? Which would be more comfortable to you?

I once talked with a graduate student who was upset about the school counselor in her building. He had a large picture of "The Last Supper," on the wall behind his chair. Further, it was the kind of holographic picture that changed as you looked at it from different angles, and the picture changed from "The Last Supper" to a large picture of "The Crucifixion" as you moved your chair. There was no doubt about his view of the world. It was inappropriate for a public school (and poor taste for a parochial school). My student worked diligently to have it changed.

Solo practitioners may not have much in the way of a waiting room or reception area. If you are in the waiting room of a private practitioner, how comfortable are you sitting there? Can you hear anything that is going on in adjacent offices? Is it a place where you would begin to relax if you were a client? If there are books or magazines present, do they say anything about the counselor?

If you are a new client, the first meeting with a counselor can be very important. People tend to form first impressions quickly, and what happens in the first session may determine if the client will return for a second session and may shape the attitude the client brings to the first and subsequent sessions about his or her willingness to work on issues. First impressions can have an effect on counselors as well.

First sessions frequently include some kind of background information sheet. Some counselors will have the client fill out the sheet before they ever meet; others will use the first session as a time when the counselor may use an information sheet as a kind of session guide to help get acquainted with the client and to provide basic information on what the client wants to see the counselor about. Still other counselors will avoid written questionnaires or background information sheets in order to let the initial session be as unencumbered as possible.

Counselors will usually provide clients with information about themselves in the initial session. In fact, some state license regulations may require that the counselor provide certain information to the client in the initial session. This written or printed material is sometimes called a *professional disclosure* sheet. The content may vary from counselor to counselor and the requirement may vary from state to state, but it usually contains information about fees, method of payment, what happens if you miss an appointment, emergency contact information, limits of confidentiality, counseling philosophy, perhaps some descriptions of what the therapy sessions might include in terms of certain techniques or counselor behaviors, and what the client is to do if he or she has a complaint against the counselor. Other matters about who maintains records and who has access to records or test data are often included.

The major process that all counselors use with clients is to listen. The shape and direction of the questions they raise and the way they respond to statements clients make may be directed by the particular philosophy of counseling they utilize in working with clients, but listening, questioning, and reflecting what has been said will be the primary behaviors of the counselor in the first and subsequent sessions.

The number of sessions the counselor and client will have depend on several things including the nature of the presenting problem and how the counselor and client will define success or goal attainment, the manner in which the client comes to the counselor, and the method of payment. In reverse order, payment method may be limited to a certain number of sessions as defined by the insurer or the agent paying for the counseling sessions. If the client is coming to a counselor because of a work-related issue, perhaps a supervisor conflict or an employee-employee conflict, then the sending agency might have a contract that limits the number of sessions for that kind of situation. Other kinds of counseling programs might limit the number of sessions before referral to a different kind of therapist is required. As initially stated, the nature of the presenting problem may define the number of sessions with a counselor—deep-rooted personality issues may result in years of sessions; interpersonal conflicts or situational crises may be resolved in just a few sessions.

A counseling session with a private practitioner usually involves just the counselor and the client. It might be two clients if the situation involves couples counseling, or it could be a family. In some instances, the counselor might meet with two coworkers or two persons who are in conflict and wish to have the counselor help them resolve their conflict.

What happens in the counseling session is private and confidential; however, there are limits to confidentiality, and there are times when what happens in the counseling session is known by other people. For example, nearly every counselor has at least one person who is identified as their supervisor. The counselor should meet with the supervisor on a regular basis to discuss cases and to make certain that sticky issues or dilemmas the counselor has with a particular client are being handled correctly. The supervisor functions as a kind of counselor to the counselor. What they discuss is confidential.

State mandatory reporting laws define the conditions which must be reported, the professionals who are required to report, and the penalties for professionals who do not report instances or incidents of suspected abuse. These are situations such as suspicion of child abuse, which, if suspected, the therapist is required to report. In private practice settings, practitioners need to have their reporting lines clearly established. In agency settings, the person or persons to whom the therapist reports is known in advance and procedures are established in advance on what records are made, who makes them, where they are kept, who has access to them, and what happens to both the therapist and the client or suspected victim at each step. Failure to report suspected cases, as defined by state laws, is usually a misdemeanor or possibly a felony.

Another kind of relationship the counselor might have outside of the counseling session would be a supervision group. Many counselors have a group of other professionals with whom they meet on a regular basis to discuss cases. Much like what happens with an individual supervisor, the counselor's goal in a supervision group is to make certain that appropriate techniques are being used and that the counselor is not letting personal issues get in the way of effective work with a client. This group allows counselors to have a professional colleague group who can provide constructive feedback to the counselor on what is happening.

The professional disclosure sheet that the counselor usually provides a new client will explain the nature of a supervision relationship. Information about clients is usually not discussed in supervision by name; rather, counselors discuss cases in generalities. Confidentiality is maintained, even in supervision.

There are certain times when the information from a counseling session is reported to others by specific name and situation. Those times are when a person has been sent to a counselor for evaluation by some agency—for example, an employer or potential employer, the court, or a social service agency. In those instances, the counselor will be clear with the person that what they discuss and what the counselor's findings are will be reported to the appropriate agency. In the counselor's words, the person is not the client; the sending agency is the client. That information will be made clear, but it is sometimes confusing to persons who have had experiences with counselors when they believe they are the client and they expect the guidelines of confidentiality to apply to them.

The private practitioner's work day can be flexible. There is no rule that it begins at 9 A.M. and ends at 5 P.M. The counselor will establish a work schedule that is mutually compatible with the times clients are available. This may mean that the counselor works during evenings on certain days or that he or she has office hours on weekends. A continuing dilemma for private practitioners, particularly solo practitioners, is what to do for days off, vacation time, or time away for other activities. Because of the nature of counseling, you cannot call in a substitute easily. In addition, taking time away when you are self-employed means that income is reduced—self-employed counselors do not have paid vacation time.

Being away from a practice usually means finding other counselors who provide emergency backup for critical cases. Counselors who are in a group practice have an easier time of making these arrangements. Solo practitioners have more work to do in establishing those arrangements.

Independent practitioners in the human services or mental health services generally use the basic principles of psychology and the related social sciences in order to work with individuals and small groups of persons who need some kind of assistance to resolve interpersonal conflicts, develop personal goals, gain understanding about their current and future situations in life, make decisions about life situations, find responses to personal trauma they experienced, or any other life situations people experience. Practitioners use methods and techniques that have been developed based on a theoretical premise about how people function in life.

SATISFACTIONS AND STRESSORS

There are many sources of satisfaction for counselors who work in private practice. They have the satisfaction of being with persons who are struggling to resolve personal issues or conflicts or dilemmas of some kind. Counselors get to see those persons reach some point of resolution to the condition that brought them to the counselor in the first place. Clients often leave their counseling sessions feeling much better than when they began, and they often will give the counselor credit for assisting them to reach desired goals.

There are also stressors in the work of private practitioners. Much of what they do they must keep to themselves. They cannot leave their counseling office and tell the first five persons they meet that they just helped Mr. Jones reach a decision about whether to change jobs or remain in a position that is not fulfilling. There is also the stress associated with knowing that you are working with people who are often teetering on the edge of mental health, and it is impossible, at times, to know whether what you do as a counselor helps the person tip to the side of health or fall on the side of a more serious mental condition.

Counseling has very few direct correlations between action and success or action and failure. Counselors and clients work together to achieve personal goals. The counselor's working philosophy may also say that whatever the client achieves, it is the client's accomplishment; thus, the counselor does not have success in counseling, the client does.

In Chapter 13, "Profiles," Todd Noble is quoted as saying, "If counselors are people who need to see visible signs of success from their work, then they should build houses." Todd worked for a long time in crisis management services for a county mental health agency and points out that it is one aspect of counseling which has immediate tangible results coming from the counselor's work.

If private practice is in your future, good wishes. In order to help you prepare for interviews with private practitioners while you are making your decisions, use the following interview guideline. Be sure to modify the interview guide to fit your own needs and to fit the situation(s) you encounter as you continue to collect data about the career that lies ahead of you.

INTERVIEW GUIDE FOR PRIVATE PRACTICE COUNSELORS

1. Study the Yellow Pages and other professional listings in one or two cities in states where you think you would like to live. Make a list of the following:
   a. Professional titles of persons who practice counseling and therapy as private practitioners or independent practitioners
   b. Educational degrees listed by practitioners
   c. License or certificate names listed by practitioners
2. Select persons from your lists whom you would like to interview or about whom you want additional information.
3. Select particular licenses and certificates about which you want additional information.
   a. Obtain information on each license or certificate you are interested in by doing a Web search to include *state name, license name,* and "license" (e.g., Oregon counselor license) or name of the certificate (e.g., certified addictions counselor) or name of the license (e.g., licensed psychologist).
   b. Collect information on requirements for each specialty in each state where you think you might want to live and work.
4. Develop an informational interview outline you can use with a private practitioner. Put your questions in a priority order in case you have a shorter interview time than you would like.

5. Call one or two private practitioners to request an informational interview. Ask for a specific number of minutes, and ask if it will be OK to record the informational interview. Be well prepared.
6. Be on time for your informational interview.
   a. Introduce yourself, explain your purpose, and ask for permission to take notes or to record the interview.
   b. Use your own interview outline or adapt from the following:
      (1) How did you choose this profession?
      (2) What education is required and how did you choose where you would obtain your education?
      (3) What is the licensing or certification process like? What do you have to do to maintain your license (continuing education)?
      (4) What is the most satisfying aspect of your work? What is the most dissatisfying aspect of your work?
      (5) How many clients do you typically see in a week?
      (6) What other kinds of professional work do you do in addition to seeing clients?
      (7) What do you think I should know or do as I consider entering this professional field?
      (8) What else should I know?
   c. Thank the person for the interview and ask if the recorded interview can be shared with your colleagues.
7. Make a list of the colleges or universities you think you might want to attend.
   a. Determine if the school offers a degree or preparation program in the area of your interest. (You can most likely find this information on the school's Web site.)
   b. Determine what the admissions requirements and the admission schedule are for the program of your interest.
   c. Schedule an interview with an admissions person to learn as much as you can about the program of your interest.
      (1) How many people apply and are admitted each term or each cycle?
      (2) How many people graduate on schedule, and how many eventually complete a preparation program?
      (3) How many graduates apply for and obtain licensing in the program of your interest?
      (4) How many graduates obtain employment in positions related to the degree or program emphasis?

     (5) What accreditation does the program have (double check against the catalog listing)?

  d. Do additional interviews with other universities or colleges if it seems appropriate for you.

7
COACHING AND CONSULTING

In recent years, the word *coaching* has become more popular among human service workers in business, education, and industry. Numerous persons who work as counselors in private practice have added coaching to their repertoire of techniques and procedures for work with individuals and groups. In some instances, counselors have taken up the term *coach* in its entirety and no longer use the word *counselor* in their private or independent practice.

Consultants have been available to the business world for a longer period of time. The practices of coaching and consulting are grouped in this chapter because there is a great deal that is similar between the two professions. In much of this chapter, I will use the phrase *coaching and consulting* or I will write about *consulting or coaching*. Similarly, I might write about *coach* in one paragraph and *consultant* in another. Where the two professional groups have distinctive differences, I will try to point those out.

In Chapter 13, you will find one profile for a counselor who has become a performance and executive coach (Victoria Kandt). Another profile is for a counselor (Bree Hayes) who has a long experience record as a consultant and who now is president and chief executive officer of a virtual consulting firm—The Hayes Group. Coaching at their firm is something they do with individual clients or with clients in a business group in addition to more conventional business consulting activities.

The professional behaviors of both a coach and a consultant might appear similar to the casual observer. Both persons are hired by either an individual or a company to accomplish a particular task: in the case of a performance coach, to work with an individual in order to help him or her improve performance in the individual's particular work setting. Consultants are more likely hired to address larger issues within an organization, although they might work directly in one-on-one relationships with employees in order to help them overcome some obstacle that is getting in the way of goal attainment.

Coaches, in general, are more likely to work with an individual with a focus on the immediate situation—what some would refer to as "the here and now." A coach might meet with an individual and inquire what goal the individual is trying to reach. Work then continues with the individual to identify obstacles to reaching that goal, and then to develop strategies with the individual that would help him or her reach the goal. Between personal meetings with a client, a coach might be in phone or e-mail contact with the client to provide encouragement and additional strategies for attaining desired results.

Consultants frequently meet with a larger group of persons in a company or organization and then help the organization identify systemic issues that limit the organization's effectiveness. The consultant's job might end at that point, or the consultant's contract could be such that work continues with persons in the organization to overcome the obstacles and reach desired goals. In doing that, a consultant might schedule meetings with individuals or the consultant might meet with groups of people in the organization to deliver focused training on some issue that was determined to be needed by groups of people in the organization. For example, consultants might conduct training sessions on diversity issues, how to improve customer relations, or conduct motivation sessions.

Coaches can be hired by individuals for specific jobs—finding ways to organize materials so that the person's desk appears neat and orderly and paperwork is handled a minimum number of times. Or, coaches might be hired to work with several people at the same level in a company to improve communication skills and thus enhance customer relations. Consultants might do the same thing. A coach might be hired by an individual or by a company to work with an employee who needs to make some change or improvement in work behavior identified through performance evaluations. Consultants might be hired by a company to help assess a group of employees for possible promotions or to recommend which person out of a group of applicants might be the best hire.

Both Victoria Kandt and Bree Hayes, who have background degrees in counseling, said that they use family systems theory a lot in their work. In one illustration, Bree Hayes described how she worked with a company after a merger of two other companies—each with decidedly different corporate cultures. She points out in her profile that it was like two families coming together. Victoria Kandt, in my interview with her, also pointed out that family systems theory helped her understand how groups of people within a single company develop unique relationships with each other—some of which may not be particularly helpful to the accomplishment of company goals.

There are a variety of words used as adjectives to modify both *consultant* and *coach*. If you check the professional listings in several phone books, you will probably be able to make a long list of specific job titles for each.

At present, there are few formal preparation programs designed to lead to coaching. Being a consultant has generally been a specialty that has come out of schools of business, psychology programs, and engineering or business management. If you do a Web search for *coach training,* you will be taken to several Web sites that describe certification and licensing programs for various coaching specialties. There is a federation of programs that give coach training—the International Coach Federation (ICF).

In counseling, psychology, and social work, preparation programs have been in place for many years, and there are separate accreditation programs for each. In fact, because of the age of preparation programs, there are even accreditation programs for the accreditation programs. Coaching is too young a specialty to have that kind of distinction; therefore, the person interested in becoming a coach needs to study preparation materials very carefully in order to make the best decision about whether or not to enter a program.

Some coach training programs require the entrant to have an existing graduate degree. Others do not. Counseling is a logical background preparation program for both coaching and consulting.

Coaches and consultants may work alone in solo practice or be part of large firms with many employees in similar categories. In Bree Hayes's profile (Chapter 13), she describes working for several years for an extremely large consulting firm. Victoria Kandt started her own coaching company and is truly a solo entrepreneur.

Working for either a large company or for yourself has some differences. When Bree Hayes worked for RHR International, two-thirds of her consultation pay was kept by the company. Of course, the company was making arrangements for her work, determining her travel schedule, covering her medical insurance and other benefits, and providing an established company reputation. For Victoria Kandt, one dissatisfying component of her job is that she has to constantly market herself—clients and contracts are developed by her, and a lot of work goes into preparation of proposals for work. She is always mindful of the fact that she needs to pay herself and cover her own benefits, social security payments, taxes, health insurance, and the like. Taking a day off means loss of pay.

Some people have a strong entrepreneurial spirit and relish operating alone or being the director of several persons under their employ. Other people like to have the security of being an employee in a large firm where there is less need to constantly be attuned to the details of work. Solo employees and members of large groups balance different values for those things that make them happy in their work.

If either coaching or consultation is in your future, you have a great deal of flexibility in the way you prepare for that professional specialty. I encourage you to be vigorous in carrying out several informational interviews in order to determine whether or not this is a route you want to pursue.

Good wishes.

8

COUNSELING IN GOVERNMENTAL
AND AGENCY SETTINGS

Many counselors work in governmental agencies or for other organizations that serve people in a variety of ways. What counselors in governmental agencies do often looks exactly like what persons in private or independent practice might do—the difference frequently is that the counselor in a governmental agency is more likely on a salary rather than having income based just on the number of clients or number of clock hours of service provided. The client groups might also differ in that a majority of governmental agencies that serve people tend to be involved with persons with less annual income or persons without medical insurance that would cover payment of fees for a counselor in private practice.

Many communities and most counties have health departments that include mental health services. Counselors are employed in those agencies to serve persons with a full range of mental health conditions. Other components of public health programs might be focused on a particular age range or a particular condition or need. Some counselors, for example, might work with programs that serve children in the preschool years. They might be located in a central building, and clients (children or families) come to the agency in order for children to be assessed and for families to receive counseling services to help them be better parents. In a different county, counselors might travel from one child-care center to another to deliver services on site. Children who are determined to have more severe developmental or psychological issues could also receive treatment from various mental health professionals in that same setting, or they might be referred to services in other settings.

Other counseling professionals might travel to see clients and their families in settings away from a central facility. Whether counselors travel to see clients or the other way around often depends on the size of the county or governmental unit that sponsors the service. You can probably find a long list of these professionals and the agencies within which they work by checking directories in the phone book.

Other examples of counseling programs in governmental agencies can be found by checking the listings in your phone book. When I open the "Community Service" pages of my local phone book, there are two pages of two-column listings beginning with "Alcohol/Drug Abuse" and ending with "YMCA" where many counseling professionals work.

In Chapter 13 that contains profiles of persons who hold different counseling or related positions, there are five people who have worked or currently work for a governmental agency—Tom Eversole, Scott Christie, Bree Hayes, Todd Noble, and Allan Mandell. Tom Eversole worked as a counselor with adolescents in a county treatment facility and later became the health director for a county health department that had over 100 staff members. Scott Christie has worked as a therapist and supervisor in a county mental health unit, as has Allan Mandell, who currently works as manager of mental health services for a county. Todd Noble spent 14 years working in a county mental health organization, ending up as the manager of crisis services. Bree Hayes was working for a community mental health agency when she developed her first contract to provide outreach services, which later morphed into a business venture as she organized a consulting company.

Most of the people who have worked in governmental mental health organizations at the county level or other, will talk about the satisfaction of being able to deliver services to people who are truly in need. They will also talk about the frustrations of seeing funding patterns change with different legislatures and with the vagaries of economic times. Several of the five persons mentioned above indicated that working for county or state agencies has put them in a position to have direct influence on policy decisions and legislative matters that subsequently impact large numbers of people—a satisfying activity.

Mental health work for governmental agencies is also available to persons on a contract basis. Often, counties or governmental units will issue contracts for persons to provide certain mental health services for a designated population and for a designated period of time. Frequently these are contracts developed as a result of special funds available for a limited amount of time. For example, a state might issue a call for proposals to provide mental health and child development services to pre-school children in a rural setting as part of an effort to have children be ready to enter school and to assist families in good parenting practices. Counselors who work in those kinds of programs—providing individual and group training and therapy with both children and parents—may get a lot of satisfaction from their work and then a lot of frustration when funds are cut or funding priorities shift to a different age group or a different method of delivering service.

Some governmental counseling positions can be very short term and focused. For example, in my city, in an effort to deal with the homeless population more effectively, the city hired one person for the summer to be on the streets and to work with the homeless population. That person's task is to do very informal assessments to determine persons in need of more intensive mental health services, to assist persons in finding the appropriate referral agencies and resources for which they are eligible, and to build a trust relationship with persons who are homeless in order to assist them as needs arise.

In Todd Noble's profile in Chapter 13, he describes his responsibilities as director of crisis services as doing assessments and then getting people to appropriate treatment. In his words, he said he was trying to get them "hooked on hope." Quick assessments may be a large part of the job of many counselors and mental health workers in governmental agencies. Many people who work for governmental agencies see clients in desperate need. The clients may be in difficult financial circumstances, have inadequate housing, have no health insurance, and may have experienced a long history of employment, health, and personal difficulties. They are often challenging populations to work with in the mental health arena; however, they also provide some of the most rewarding work situations because they are people for whom a bit of assistance may result in large changes in their lives—something that may not be as visible if one is working with affluent clients in a selective independent practice.

Counselors in governmental agencies often have an additional responsibility related to the clients they serve. It is common for them to have membership on planning or study committees that are looking for solutions to issues related to particular populations—for example, a counselor in a county mental health agency might be a regular member of a community group attempting to find solutions to conditions experienced by persons who are homeless. Or, a counselor who works with preschool children might also work with planning groups that have those same children as their area of concern. The counselor might be expected to come to those meetings representing a body of information other members do not have and to be able to assist in policy development or in finding strategies to implement for best solutions.

Counselors might also be called on to make public presentations on issues related to their work. A counselor from a state or county agency may be asked to speak to civic clubs, fund-raising groups, or other organizations that study population issues. In Chapter 13, several of the counselors talked about their activities testifying to legislative committees and to licensing agencies at the time that changes were under consideration. One counselor spoke with great pleasure about his efforts to influence a legislative committee by using his extensive experience as a counselor in a county mental health agency. He commented that working with a client felt good, but that having an influence on a piece of legislation that would impact thousands of clients felt even better.

You can explore the opportunities for counseling or mental health positions in the community you think you would want to live in by checking the governmental Web sites that relate to your areas of interest—state, county, city, or specialized agency. Look in the personnel groupings for the titles of positions available and for the titles of positions normally staffed in the agency. Use that list to select a person (or persons) with whom you would like to conduct an informational interview to learn more about being a counselor in a governmental agency.

GUIDELINES FOR AN INFORMATIONAL INTERVIEW

1. Scan the government pages of your local phone book to identify city, county, and state agencies that employ counselors and other mental health workers.
2. Check the Web sites of those agencies to see what counseling positions are named.
3. Do a Web search for counseling or mental health services in the communities in which you think you would like to live and work.
4. Check with the personnel office or the human relations officer for the governmental unit you are interested in to determine if you can obtain copies of position descriptions for the titles that interest you.
5. Check the licensing and certification requirements for your positions of interest. Check those requirements with your educational program for a match.
6. Make an appointment with one or more persons working in a counseling position.

7. Be prepared for the interview time they give you. Develop your own interview questions, perhaps including some of the following:
   a. How would you describe a typical day or week in your job?
   b. What are the advantages and disadvantages of working for a governmental agency such as this?
   c. What are the most satisfying and the most distressing things about your job?
   d. Where did you receive your preparation? Do you have recommendations about what I should be doing in a preparation program if I want this kind of job?
   e. How stable or secure is your job? What does that depend on?
   f. What else should I know about this kind of position? And are there other persons you would recommend that I talk with?
8. Be sure to thank the person for the interview and follow up with a written thank you.

9

COUNSELING IN SPECIAL SETTINGS AND WITH SPECIAL POPULATIONS

THE ELECTRONIC AND INTERNET AGE

The electronic age has introduced several new counseling procedures. Most are new enough that effectiveness research has not been collected to the extent that the new methods can be described as successful or not.

Two of the most frequently discussed electronic counseling processes are counseling by use of the telephone and counseling via the Internet. With the rapidly growing popularity of Web cams and telephone links to computer images, the two procedures meld into a third form—counseling via Web-transmitted voice and image.

Use of the telephone and written exchanges have a fairly long history in the areas of providing personal assistance with difficult issues. Letter writing has long been a means of exploring deep personal issues. Phone calls are famous for what they have provided people in times of trouble. Both letter writing and telephone exchange have been the subject of novels, movies, and television shows that demonstrate a variety of situations where one person communicates with another to seek help with some issue.

The value of writing, just getting troubling thoughts on paper, has been a long-standing therapeutic technique, and there are many people who talk about the value of journaling. Clients do not always have to be sitting in an office across from a therapist in order to work on substantive issues. The immediacy and accessibility that the telephone and text messaging provide certainly introduce a unique concept to mental health work. One of the most commonly accepted in the electronic counseling arena would be the operation of crisis-call centers. Public bulletin boards, newspapers, magazine advertisements, and television spot commercials are filled with public service announcements listing phone numbers for suicide hotlines, sexual assault hotlines, homeless teen contact numbers, gambling addiction call centers, and numerous other topical call centers. The world of the "800-number" help line is commonly accepted among counseling professionals, with many counselors providing training to volunteers who answer those hotline calls or providing supervision and referral links for callers.

Many counselors have been reluctant to undertake counseling via electronic media. Chapter 7 references the use of the telephone as a common tool of executive coaches. In an historically related process, the exchange of letters—even by slow postage systems—has existed for many years as a means of two people working through personal issues with use of written exchange. Electronic communication has merely extended that process to the instantaneous mode of modern day.

Electronic counseling presents several questions for the profession, and there are task forces and groups in each of the major counseling professional associations who are at work trying to resolve the related issues. On the list of thorny questions are the issues of (a) licensing, (b) certification or other credentialing, (c) supervision, (d) records and security, (e) development of standards of care, and (f) payment for service.

Licensing presents an immediate issue. Because licenses for counseling services are controlled by states, how does licensing apply if the counselor is in one state and the client in another? Even more fundamental is the question of what kind of license is required for a person to function as a counselor? Nearly all the counseling theories and techniques studied in graduate schools have been developed on face-to-face counseling applications. What changes in those theories and techniques are required to make them be applicable in long-distance situations?

Licenses for any occupation are designed, in part, to provide the consumer—in this case, a client—with a means of making a complaint or of getting some response to poor or inappropriate service. If a telephone counseling client lives in one state and the counselor lives in another, what recourse does the client have if he or she wishes to file a formal or legal complaint? This is the kind of question that professional associations and state licensing groups currently struggle with as the field of electronic counseling expands.

Certification is a related matter. From our previous discussions of certification, you know that almost anyone can establish a training or educational program of some kind, and upon completion, can award the participants certification in some designated topic or process. There

are no standard requirements on the number of contact hours participants must complete, and there is no standard definition of the content requirements for certificates. I might present a 4-hour workshop
to interested participants, at the end of which each could be presented
with a certificate naming them a "certified telephone counselor" or a
"certified videoconferencing counselor." As the tendency to offer telephone or video counseling services expands, there will no doubt be
accompanying demands to develop definitions, standards, and evaluative processes for electronic psychological services. It is not there yet.

There have been a few studies about the effectiveness of providing
supervision for counselors via telephone, Web chat rooms, and videoconferencing. Supervision of telephone counseling is still an unknown area.

The client of a telephone or videoconferencing service should have
some questions about the security of the transmissions and the safety
and security of any records transmitted. Counselors generally assume
that the standard guidelines for collection, maintenance, transmission,
and destruction of client records, which apply in face-to-face counseling situations also apply to electronic counseling procedures. Clients
would be well advised to inquire about record procedures if they choose
that method of interpersonal work.

All of the questions and issues identified in the paragraphs above
become just the tip of the iceberg for the professions in development
of standards of care the professional counselor uses to label his or her
practice. Other specialties may be identified in the wording of professional listings in the Yellow Pages or among the lists of counselors found
in Internet searches, lists included in the resource directories published
in many communities, and in announcements in daily or in alternative
newspaper publications.

Some counseling specialties are associated with the setting or institution where the counselor works. Other specialties may be identified
by the locale in which the counseling takes place. Most specialties are
identified based on the target population the counselor serves. The following section provides some information about a number of different
counseling specialties.

COUNSELING SPECIALTIES BY SETTING

Prisons and Jails

Many counselors work with persons who are at some stage in the judicial system. Counselors might work with persons after arrest and before
trial—especially with juveniles who are just entering the elaborate

judicial system. Counselors might be known just as *counselors*; however, other labels might be used—offender counselor, juvenile counselor, or youth counselor. Following trial and conviction, if that occurs, counselors might have the additional label of *probation* or *parole* placed on their titles, and they might work with juveniles and adults who are incarcerated or who are in the community awaiting additional court procedures.

There are professional associations to which counselors belong who work with clients who are at some stage of the judicial system—the Public Offender Counselor Association (POCA) is one of those groups. They provide a place for offender counselors to meet and continue to work on skill sets that apply to their specialty.

One of the major difficulties facing any counselor who works with clients in the judicial system is the question (both for the client and the counselor) of who the counselor is really working for. In other words, who is the client? It is most probable that the client sees the counselor as an extension of the court, and this may make the client reluctant to develop a close working relationship with the counselor. On the other side of the desk, the counselor may present as totally committed to the client but then discovers information that would be important for the court to have. These are common dilemmas for persons on both sides of criminal cases.

If counselors are assigned by the court to do assessments and make recommendations about clients, then that role is usually clear to both counselor and client; however, it is always possible that during a court-mandated assessment, the counselor discovers information that is problematic in terms of knowing what to do with it. If the counselor has been retained by attorneys for one side or the other in court assessment situations, it is often easier for the counselor to resolve what to do with information discovered through the interview process—although not always.

Counselors who work with persons who are incarcerated must work through their own issues about being inside locked facilities. Nearly everyone who works in a prison or jail will describe the feelings they had the first time they went through security and heard that door slam shut behind them. Some of the feeling lingers, even for those who work "inside" for a long time.

Another issue for counselors who work inside is that their clients might suddenly be moved from one facility to another without much notice. The person's status might change quickly because of some incident that happened that they may or may not have been a part of, resulting in the counselor having access to a person one week and not the next. On the other hand, counselors who work with some convicted persons who have been in the same facility for years and who anticipate being there much longer may represent one of the most stable client populations that any counselor will ever work with.

Because most counselors who work with persons in the judicial system are ultimately employed by governmental units, the qualifications for their work need to be obtained from the employing units. Interested persons should check state, county, city, and private corporation Web sites to find position titles, position descriptions, qualification lists, and application processes for the various counseling positions available.

Counseling in Military Installations

A variety of counseling positions exist in the various elements of military installations. In the uniformed military units, the most frequent image that comes to mind for counselors would be the military chaplain who might be on the battlefield under fire or in a church, synagogue, mosque, or temple on a military base. In addition, there are nonuniformed counseling positions attached to nearly every military unit of any size.

Counselors in the military might work with military families and dependents. They might work with uniformed military. They are frequently found in military hospitals and rehabilitation units. The work of counselors in the military can depend a lot on the stage of the military personnel with whom they work. For example, military personnel with many years of service who are approaching retirement often have programs available to them to assist in making the transition from military life to civilian life. Civilian and military personnel (counselors) might work with individuals and groups in a series of programs to assist with those transitions.

In units where uniformed military are deployed overseas for long periods of time, the families and dependents frequently face difficult issues for which counselors can provide valuable assistance. Military personnel often refer to a person's MOS (Military Occupation Specialty). Persons interested in finding the full array of counseling positions related to the military should examine what those are and what the qualifications are by exploring the topics in an Internet search or by inquiring at a military recruitment office.

In a time of military conflict, there is always an escalation in the number of uniformed military personnel who are injured. This situation places a high demand on people trained in rehabilitation counseling. Information from the American Rehabilitation Counseling Association can be helpful for an interested reader. Another professional association that relates to counselors in the military is the Association for Counselors and Educators in Government (ACEG). This organization was formerly named the Military Educators and Counselors Association and can provide good information about counselors in the military.

One additional counseling specialty often associated with military installations is for counselors working in the area of addictions. In an effort to retain military personnel rather than have to discharge them from service, there has been a tendency for the military to find treatment systems for persons wrestling with addictions. Some larger military installations will have professional and semiprofessional specialists who work with impaired personnel as well as design and implement addiction prevention programs.

As is the case for counselors working in the judicial system, there may be times when counselors in the military have struggles identifying who really is the client—the uniformed personnel or the military unit. Counselors and military personnel should be alert to these possible conflicts.

Veterans' Hospitals

At the close of World War II, the field of counseling psychology received a tremendous boost of energy in a growth spurt similar to the post-Sputnik and National Defense Education Act (NDEA) impetus on improved school counseling. The flood of veterans returning home with veteran's benefits available to them demanded an improved brand of counseling service in order to assist in transitions from military to civilian life, rehabilitation of war-related injuries and traumas, and selection of educational and career options. Counseling services in the VA hospitals have continued as a core component of veteran benefits.

In current times, veterans returning from battlefields in Iraq, Afghanistan, and other theaters of operation bring a new set of traumas and injuries that require intensive rehabilitation and specially trained counselors and therapists. Various estimates of the long-term psychological damage of contemporary battle conditions have produced huge numbers in terms of the number of years into the future, which will see emerging and continuing effects of battle experiences. Technical advances in battlefield medical treatment have resulted in entirely new sets of medical conditions for counselors and psychologists to work with in the veteran populations they serve. For example, the Vietnam War has been over for a number of years, but VA facilities continue to diagnose new cases of posttraumatic stress disorder (PTSD) among veterans who only now are finding out why work, family, and other life processes have been so difficult to manage. The long-term effect of Iraq and Afghanistan, not to mention the immediate effect, will be enormous.

The new forms of counseling and therapy required to serve this population with its new set of war-related effects is just now emerging.

Addictions Counseling

One form of counseling practice that has seen an increase in demand in recent years is addictions counseling. There are numerous addictions and addiction groups that utilize counseling services—some by individual choice and some by court mandate. The addictions model most commonly known to the general public follows the Alcoholics Anonymous (AA) 12-Step model and related programs for narcotics addiction (NA), gambling addiction (GA), or sexual addiction (SAA) can be found in most communities with meeting times and locations announced in the classified ads of newspapers or posted in prominent places. The 12-Step AA model operates as a self-monitored group, and no specially trained counselor is required for the group to function.

Other addiction groups may function more like a group counseling program with a trained, certified, or licensed facilitator. One or the other of the addictions treatment models may be used by the court as requirements in sentencing when a person's legal difficulties have been tied to one of the addictions. As a result, some states have found ways to fund addiction-treatment programs; the result is that there is a demand in some locales for counselors with special addiction treatment specialization.

Counselors who work in the area of addictions often have two major issues to deal with related to their work—one is that they often work with reluctant clients who are with them only because the court or someone (perhaps a partner, spouse, or employer) has said that it is a requirement; the other is that it is difficult to find high success rates among persons with addictions who are in treatment. If counselors need to see visible signs of success from the work they do, addictions counseling may be a difficult specialty to be in. Similarly, if counselors have a hard time working with a client group that begins its contact with you by saying, "I don't want to be here and I don't need to be here," then this field of work may not be personally rewarding.

Numerous listings of professional counselors in a community will include persons who advertise addictions counseling as one of their specialties. As private practitioners who so label themselves, they are more likely to find the client who comes to a session saying that he or she has a problem and wants to work through it. Private practitioners have more latitude in saying they will or will not take on a client based on his or her initial willingness to work on change.

Rehabilitation Counseling

Another specialty in counseling is in rehabilitation work. The scope of rehabilitation counselors is wide, with work similar to that already described with veterans or persons dealing with addictions. In addition, rehabilitation counselors often work in the area of work-related injuries and assess a person's ability to resume work after an illness or injury as well as assist persons to find appropriate adaptive measures that enable them to have success in various areas of their life.

There are professional associations for rehabilitation counselors. The American Rehabilitation Counseling Association (ARCA) and the National Rehabilitation Counseling Association (NRCA) both work to develop standards, assure quality preparation, and refine the theory and practice of rehabilitation counseling. There are also certification and accreditation programs for rehabilitation counselors and for preparation programs. In addition, states license rehabilitation counselors.

Rehabilitation counselors work in a variety of different settings—in private practice, in hospitals and rehabilitation centers, in schools and governmental agencies, and in other settings where persons with some physical or mental limitation require that adaptations be made for them to function at their best.

Special Topic Centers

Counselors work in a number of different kinds of centers, each focused on a particular target population. For example, communities might have a center that targets issues like rape and domestic violence. The services offered could range all the way from private and secure residential facilities for persons or families where domestic violence is happening to just a telephone information and referral facility operated by volunteers.

Numerous centers aimed at specific populations can be found in community listings with the number of special topic centers increasing as city populations increase. Examples would include centers for women, sexual-minority youth, homeless adults, veterans, single parents, the homeless, addicted persons, and the like. The counseling functions performed at centers of this kind are often handled by volunteers with a minimal amount of professional training. Frequently, there may be a professional counselor who provides volunteer training and supervision of the volunteer activity.

Staff members for centers such as those described above, and for many others, often rely on people who have experienced the same conditions as the clients the center is intended to serve but who have made it through their difficulties to reach some stage where they can provide assistance to others. There are many persons who believe that therapeutic relationships with persons in such centers are only established with counselors who have experienced the same conditions in their past. Professional counselors who work in special topic centers to either provide training for volunteers or to provide direct service or supervision for volunteers nearly always have the initial task of establishing credibility with the client group if they have not, at one time, been a member of the client group.

Hospice Care

A growing movement around the country is hospice care for persons in the final stages of their life. Hospice organizations operate under the aegis of various groups—hospitals, churches, and medical clinics, to name a few. They are usually staffed by combinations of paid and volunteer workers, and it is customary for both paid and volunteer staff members to undergo special training in the issues of death and dying before they actually begin their work with hospice clients.

Professional counselors are frequently included as staff members in hospice programs. Their duties often include providing training and supervision to volunteers. Those same positions are filled by clergy in many hospice programs, with some clergy having received special training in grief work, hospice issues, and supervision of volunteers. If you do an Internet search with the words *hospice* or *hospice care,* you will find numerous listings that describe the qualifications of hospice staff and the special training they receive prior to work as volunteers. If you include the terms *hospice staff certification,* you will find several examples of the kind of preparation that health care and counseling professionals go through to work in hospice.

III

This section consists of two short chapters that give the reader an overview of the job market for counselors as well as provide some strong suggestions about what to do and not do in the job search process.

Chapter 10, "Are There Jobs Out There?" addresses some of the supply and demand questions new professionals face. The reader is directed to a number of different sources that provide information about job openings. The U.S. government publications associated with the Department of Labor are referenced. These provide employment data with projections for demand as well as with salary information for many different counseling jobs. The labor department data are, by necessity, very broad in their application and do not reflect the single position in a single agency in one community. It is valuable information to study for consideration of the long-term future of the counseling professions.

Other sources for job postings and announcements of openings are mentioned in the chapter. The reader is urged to develop a systematic method of learning about the kinds of openings that fit their own specialty. These sources are often associated with professional associations. Other sources—newspaper listings, online announcements, and commercial search firms are also discussed.

The answer to the question posed in this chapter—are there jobs out there?—is "yes." The successful job applicant will have developed an effective search procedure in order to find that perfect position.

Chapter 11, "Your Application Process," presents a much more focused set of suggestions about how to find a job in the field of your choice. I included a number of real examples from my own experience of persons who were not successful in their job searches. When the kinds of blunders they made in the search process are examined, it may seem so obvious that what they did was wrong that the reader would say it would never happen to them. I hope that is true.

10
ARE THERE JOBS OUT THERE?

Are there jobs out there for me? Anyone who is serious about employment in a particular field will be asking this question at some point or another—either before, during, or following completion of a preparation program. There may be some persons who have no intention of seeking employment in one of the counseling fields. They may have entered the preparation program because it provided an interesting area of personal study, which met some of their own academic and personal development goals. Other persons may have had specific employment all lined up before they even began a preparation program: a superintendent of schools might have told them that if they get a degree, they will be promised a position as a school counselor.

For most persons, the preparation program is preparation for a position in a field, not preparation for one specific job. They are the persons who will be asking the question: "Is there a job out there for me?" The answer to that question comes from a number of different sources: information interviews, study of job listings in different professional publications, local newspapers and media, personal contacts, and the U.S. Bureau of Labor Statistics.

INFORMATION INTERVIEWS

Throughout this book, I continue to suggest informational interviews as a valuable source of many kinds of information for the person deciding on a career in one of the counseling professions. As part of any informational interview—whether with a professional counselor, a college or university preparation program, or a potential employer—the question can always be asked: "What is the current and future job market for counselors in this field?" Additionally, information interviews can provide information about issues or conditions that may impact current and future trends on both supply and demand for particular counseling positions. For example, an information interview with a professional counselor may alert you to changes in licensing laws, availability of funds for counseling programs, or changes in administrative philosophies about staffing of counseling positions.

Persons intently focused on finding employment in one specific location or in one particular institution need to pay more attention to information interviews in that location or institution than persons who know that when they complete their preparation program they will be free to move about the country in search of their ideal job. The person who knows he or she cannot easily leave his or her home community after completion of the preparation program would be well served to include questions in his or her informational interviews about forthcoming vacancies, pending retirements, planned program expansions, and probable contacts for employment following completion of their programs.

JOB LISTINGS

Job seekers can begin an early watch for the position listings that fit their own set of criteria for the position and the location of their preference. In doing the various informational interviews suggested in this book, persons can begin to find out where and in what publications the positions of interest commonly appear. In addition to typical newspaper announcements, many professional positions will be identified in the related professional publications for that particular specialty. For example, college counselor positions will be published in higher education publications such as the *Chronicle of Higher Education* and in the publications of the professional associations that include the person's specialty.

Many universities, public schools, hospitals, and other large organizations may have their own position listings, and an interested person would do well to identify those that include his or her area of interest and then get included in the regular mailings—e-mail, Web page listings, and regular print mail sources. It is important to watch the publication listings long enough in advance that you understand the schedule for announcement of position openings and closings. There is nothing quite so disheartening as to find out the day after a position has been filled that an opening existed for which you could have been an applicant.

PROFESSIONAL PUBLICATIONS

Every professional association will have procedures for listing position openings. Often, these are for national searches, but a professional counseling association might have a regional organization with its own publication in which position openings are listed. It is also typical that with each subdivision of a national publication, the time lag between announcement of a position opening and the printing or posting of that opening increases so that it is possible that the day you learn of a position opening in a regional professional publication is the day after it closed or was filled. Be alert to time lines and schedules. Use professional publication position listings over several weeks or months to become informed about the pattern of listings, the kind of listings included, and the potential sources of position openings.

NEWSPAPER AND MEDIA LISTINGS

Newspapers will carry lists of openings for counselors in a number of different professional specializations. In metropolitan areas, it is also a frequent practice for weekend issues of newspapers to have special supplements for professional positions. You should study issues for several weeks to determine the pattern of listings that focus on your own area of professional interest. Determine which classified categories include the particular positions of interest for you—*counselor* in one paper may be listed as *human service* in another.

Posting a position opening in a newspaper or on an electronic bulletin board may be a requirement of an employing organization. Those postings may appear in print several days after they have been made known through other channels—in-house bulletin boards, in-house electronic newsletters, professional association postings, or other distribution vehicles. Be sure to study the distribution processes of the area of primary interest for yourself in order to not have good position postings slip past you because of deadlines or other technical errors.

PERSONAL CONTACTS

If you were to ask a group of people at random how they obtained the first job they ever had, many would describe the process as being connected to a family member, a long-time friend, or an associate of a family member. Of course, this common method can be used to illustrate how the employed are usually connected to the employed and why it is difficult for a person from a long-term family experience of unemployment to break into the employment world.

Some of the same dynamics work in employment of persons in professional counseling positions. Referral from a personal friend, connection with a family member, or other experience from a person in a position to influence initial professional employment is effective—even in professional positions. It would be important for persons to make a list of contacts.

I once had a student who had one section of her notebook sectioned off as "contacts." She always had an eye to possible contacts and collected names and contact information for many persons whom she met through all kinds of educational, business, and social interactions. She would also make notes for the contacts about what she discussed with them, whether she identified them as a potential referral or recommending source, and enough other information that she knew she could remind that person at some later date about their interaction— even if that person did not have a good memory about what had gone on. At the time, my observation was that she was extremely well organized and tremendously effective in preparing herself to utilize the network possibilities to obtain her ideal job.

U.S. BUREAU OF LABOR STATISTICS

The most comprehensive source of information about current conditions and future trends in employment in any of the counseling professions is the U.S. Bureau of Labor Statistics. For years, the *Occupational Outlook Handbook* (*OOH*) has been the most authoritative print document on employment information. In the current technological age, the *OOH* is available at the click of a mouse.

You should check http://www.bls.gov/OCO/ and plan to spend some time with a variety of searches to learn as much as you can about the professional positions of interest to you. You will find the *OOH* an easily searchable Web site. There is nearly always a "search" box on the opening page. You can enter the name of a professional position—counselor, psychologist, social worker—and do a broad search. You can enter a more specific position title—rehabilitation counselor, school psychologist, clinical social worker—and go deeper within the information provided.

The *OOH* will take you to a number of other Web sites—addresses for professional associations related to your career title of interest, supply and demand employment projects, salary range information, licensing and certification requirements and sources for that same information, job duties, education and training requirements, and specific job information about what you would have to lift, carry, or otherwise be required to do for the health and safety of workers in that profession.

By necessity, *OOH* information is aggregated information and seldom gets down to the small unit of interest—the one job you want to apply for and obtain; however, the aggregated data will give you the best picture of the positions you have interest in of all the information sources available. In addition, information will be available on the Web sites to tell you how old the information is that you are reading.

The ease with which you can obtain information about professional positions has been central to the decision to not put that information in this book. Any dated material will be out of date by the time the first print copy is available. Students and other seekers who have access to a computer and Web searches can obtain the best information in the most current fashion with a click or two of the mouse.

At times, the *OOH* gets a little technical. Positions may be labeled with identifying codes or other abbreviations. The codes and abbreviations are important for governmental workers who compile and disseminate the information as well as for the readers who consume the information. In particular, professional positions are sometimes advertised or listed by code. This is especially true for counseling positions within governmental agencies or for agencies funded by governmental grants. If those employing sources are part of what you consider as potential for yourself, then having familiarity with occupational codes is important for you.

COMMERCIAL SOURCES

The current electronic age provides job seekers with a variety of sources for position listings as well as procedures for posting résumés and making applications. Some schools, hospitals, large organizations, and major agencies may use Web postings as the primary means of both announcing positions and accepting applications.

To my knowledge, there is no accreditation or screening procedure that would permit a potential user to determine the quality or the extent of a commercial electronic job placement service. That may be something that develops in the future. At present, I urge prospective users of public or commercial electronic employment listings to do their own research with employers. Ask the question, "Do you use any of the electronic position announcement sites, or do you consider applications from commercial electronic job postings?" (Note that I am intentionally not naming any of the electronic job boards, because the names change frequently and new ones emerge with some frequency.)

ARE THERE JOBS OUT THERE?

Yes. Jobs are out there. Your task is to find the one that comes closest to meeting your criteria for that ideal position. Your larger task is to present yourself to the employer in such a way that the employer will grab you up as the best thing to come their way in a decade. The next chapter will make some suggestions about your application process.

11

YOUR APPLICATION PROCESS

Unless you have been promised a position far in advance of the time you began your preparation program, then the process of finding that ideal job, applying for it, and securing the position requires a lot of very intentional and systematic work. During your informational interviews, you may have found someone who told you his or her story of finding a job by luck, accident, or some other fluke of timing and place. The majority of positions are found and secured by implementing a good application process.

It may be as important to have listened to people in your informational interviews tell you about job application mistakes that they have made or that they have observed in others. Collecting those "don't-do-this" anecdotes can be humorous if it is someone else and disastrous if it is you. In my own career in academia, I can easily recall a few application goofs that resulted in persons not being offered positions.

We did not invite the person to campus for an interview who sent an application that was handwritten on a legal pad, photocopied, and the name of some institution painted out with our address sloppily written on the smeared white-out. Our only question was: "Is this guy serious?"

We did not invite the person to campus who sent an application with our address on the front page and names of other institutions on subsequent pages. They were not even the same names, so the writer's initial sentence saying that we were the "only" institution to which he was applying did not quite ring true.

We did not invite the person to campus who, when I called to see about scheduling an interview based on a good set of credentials, did not recognize the name of the person he had sent the application to (me) or the location of the university, or the particulars of the position for which he was applying.

We did not offer a position to a candidate who came to the interview with no apparent knowledge of the institution, the faculty, or the programs the institution offered. Further, try as hard as we could, we did not find any interest on the person's part in wanting to know more about the institution.

We did not consider the applicant seriously who, at dinner, was the first person to speak up and order a drink: "A double scotch, no ice, and keep 'em coming."

We did not offer a position to the candidate who, during the interview, explained how he or she would discard or redesign each of the major components of the existing program, clearly indicating a lack of philosophical fit.

PLANNING YOUR APPLICATION STRATEGY

There are many books on the market in the category of job search or career finder publications. It may be a good idea to scan several of these books and pick the one or two that fit your employment objectives best. There will be different approaches suggested for persons seeking a position in higher education; different strategies for positions that required a professional license than those for unlicensed entry-level positions. Your ultimate goal is to design a résumé and an application that are so unique and effective that the desired employer will see your application as the one that must result in a hire. To do that, you need to do some work:

1. *Start early*—You need to be able to document your life experience as well as your employment history.
2. *Research potential employers*—You need a lot of knowledge about potential employers.
3. *Develop an effective résumé*—Know what the résumé requirements are for each potential employer and make yours fit their requirements.
4. *Use an editor*—Make certain that several people have reviewed your written material.
5. *Develop your references*—Make certain you have talked extensively with potential references and never have them be surprised by a request.
6. *Design a tracking system for applications*—Know what you sent, where you sent it, and when you sent it.

7. *Know the law*—Be familiar with federal and state regulations that apply to applications and interview procedures.

Start Early

The materials you put together for an application must reflect who you are—not just at the moment of application, but also for the prior months and years. The education or preparation program you completed is important; however, your other employment, your volunteer work, and your achievements in work and nonwork events may be the kind of statements a prospective employer would take special note of. You should start early—both in acquiring relevant and focused experiences and in maintaining a way to document and quantify what you have done so that it can be communicated to an interested employer in a succinct fashion.

It is helpful if you maintain or can develop a list of your relevant activities—both volunteer and work related—which will indicate what you did, when you did it, with whom you did it, and who can verify or comment on the nature of what you did. For example, a comment on an application that you "volunteered with the city park department," does not say much about you—it could be that you picked up trash after a public event. Being able to say that as a volunteer you were responsible for "directing recreational activities for a group of five adjudicated adolescent males for 20 hours a week for 3 months each of two summers" turns the word *volunteered* into a much more specific and meaningful line on an application. It tells a reader that you had substantive responsibilities and that you did the work over a period of time (hence, you must have been reliable enough to be asked back a second summer). It also says that you have experience with a population of youth some would describe as difficult and certainly speaks well of you if your interest is in one of the counseling professions that deals with young people. You can also describe the volunteer activity in terms of start and end dates and should be able to name the supervisor who could comment on all those things that a prospective employer wants to know.

I have frequently seen persons struggle in their attempts to construct both a work and volunteer history. I strongly recommend that people begin a file they can maintain somewhere with accumulated experience, being certain to include inclusive dates, position titles, a reminder of responsibilities, and contact information for a supervisor or personnel department that can verify information in your record. You may be asked to complete information for a criminal background check for many positions, and specificity about employment dates, places, and supervisors becomes very important.

Research Potential Employers

The best-qualified candidate is usually one who knows a great deal about the potential employer. Even before submitting an application for a position, and especially before any kind of interview—telephone or face-to-face—you should do a lot of homework on the employer. This may be more essential for positions where you would become a member of a working group than for those where you would function as an individual with responsibilities to and supervision by one person.

I have seen seemingly qualified candidates for positions in academia literally shoot themselves in the foot by not having knowledge (or apparent interest) in the colleagues with whom they would work, the nature of the institution, or the community or locale in which they would live or work. On the other hand, I have seen candidates go overboard on their preinterview research of an institution by being overly enthusiastic with each colleague they met and indicating they "read every word you ever wrote," or being so complimentary of their work that it almost turned people off in the middle of a conversation or an interview. It is important to know about colleagues and what they do; it is also important to know if these are colleagues with whom you could work or who would support you in your own work; however, temper your interview expressions of love and affection.

Researching institutional characteristics as part of your application process is critical. For larger organizations—schools, universities, businesses, social service groups—there are probably institutional reports available in print or online, which will provide information about employment and working conditions. Public agencies—universities, municipalities, governmental organizations—will usually have salary and compensation data available through public channels. For smaller organizations or smaller working groups, it is more difficult to obtain information about work groups or individuals. My strong recommendation for applicants to clinics or smaller work groups in one of the counseling professions is that good advance preparation for any applicant would be to do a Web search on the organization as well as on each of the persons with whom you might be in a work relationship. "Google" your prospective work colleagues.

Remember that your prospective work colleagues may "Google" you. Do you know if there is information floating around in the electronic ether that you would rather not be present or which requires some explanation? I recently was in the process of arranging to do some consulting with a church. One of the members of the church "Googled" me and discovered some activities of mine which told the member that we were not philosophically compatible. It probably was a good thing that I did not conduct the consultation with the church.

The previous paragraph should serve to alert persons who will be entering the job search that they need to know what exists electronically. It may be too late to pull some of the photos or videos or other material from Facebook, YouTube, or MySpace. Be aware of what is there so you do not get caught off guard by an embarrassing question.

Develop an Effective Résumé

You can be overwhelmed with advice on how to prepare an effective résumé. The bookstore you frequent may have several shelves just on the résumé topic. Whatever you decide to use, remember that unless it is effective, you will not make it past the initial screening process. The effectiveness has to be noticed by overworked readers in the first few seconds of their look at your résumé or you will not get the opportunity to explore any of the next steps to your ideal job.

The electronic age has introduced new elements to résumé writing and review. Some larger organizations may have application processes that require that you use a fill-in-the-blank electronic form as part of the application package. I hear people complain about these procedures because they seem to eliminate individuality and uniqueness, which some other résumé form might permit.

The electronic age has also enabled you to make changes in your résumé to fit the particular requirements of employers—one employer may want a one-page résumé; another may want supervisor names; another may want reference names and addresses; and some want only names. Of course, it is important to make certain you keep track of which word-processor file you are using for the résumé you send to a given employer. I experienced being the recipient of the wrong file from applicants. In some instances, it would not matter; but, in others, it is important to make certain you are sending what you want to send as part of an application.

Use an Editor

Use an editor for your application package. In fact, you might want to use more than one editor. "How does this application look to you?" Put the question to your colleagues as well as to a good copy editor. I once was involved in a candidate search where a reasonably impressive applicant had submitted materials filled with typographical errors. Part of the responsibility of the position for which he was applying would be the expectation of writing and publication. Not only because of the typographical errors, but in large part as a result, he was not offered the position. The interesting aftereffect of that is that I had an opportunity to share the reaction to a sloppy application with the applicant. He has since regularly shared that experience with his graduate students and has adopted the practice of using an editor on all his written work.

Double-check what you are putting in the mail. This is especially important if you are sending multiple applications with several envelopes on the table and several duplicated stacks of résumés, application letters, supporting materials, and other items. Do not have the receiving organization send your material back with a note saying "Did you mean this for us or for a different organization?"

Cultivate Your References

I have had numerous experiences over the years of being contacted by a potential employer because my name had been given as a reference. In some of those instances, I am guessing the person using my name as a reference might not have wanted to list me if we had had an opportunity to talk so that I might have said how I would want to describe him or her if asked.

The first reason for working in advance to develop your references is common courtesy. The issue goes beyond a simple request, "May I list you as a reference?" That serves the courtesy aspect. The second, and perhaps more important, step is to discuss with your potential reference not only if he or she would be willing to reply if contacted by a potential employer, but to have the kind of discussion that lets you know how he or she would describe you, what perceptions he or she has about you, what supporting evidence he or she has about your work, whether he or she understands your career goals and aspirations, and how what he or she has to say will balance or complement what others would have to say whom you may list as references.

The person you ask to be a reference who says to you, "You need to understand what I would say about you. If, after hearing that, you still decide to use me as a reference, then I'm willing to do that; however, the decision rests with you." I made that statement to people over the years. Some have chosen not to use me, and others have.

Make certain that your references offer a balanced view of your life. Having all your references come from the same group of persons is not the best. Having persons outside your intended area of expertise be references is acceptable if you have others who can speak to your professional skills. Make certain that you have current information among your references.

Sometimes, screening committees will look at a list of references, and the result is that they flag questions about you which your résumé may not cover. For example, if you have just invested 2 years of graduate study in a preparation program and there is no reference listed from the program of study, questions will be raised. If all your references are over 5 years old, there will be questions. If all your references are connected to social relationships rather than work or education relationships, there will be questions.

Employing groups may request references in one of several different forms—just names and contact information for a potential reference, written letters included as part of the application packet, standardized information questionnaires that are sent by you or the employer to a reference, and direct contact by phone or e-mail. You need to discuss each of these procedures with your potential reference and ask if he or she is willing to respond to each. Some references may not wish to provide you with the letter they would write; others may only be willing to respond to direct phone calls. Know what your reference is willing to do.

How confidential are your reference materials? Several years ago, federal legislation was passed which made all kinds of records open and accessible to applicants which, in previous times, would have been closed. Most application processes will explain to applicants how their records, letters of reference, and other documents will be treated. If they do not, you are entitled to ask who will see your file and what will happen to it after the application process. The open records issue has been discussed frequently with respect to letters of recommendation. You should include this in your discussion with any potential reference. In addition, because your letters of recommendation will, in nearly all cases, be open to you, if there is an error in statement of fact, you should feel free to correct that error—both with the receiving agency and with the person who wrote the original letter.

Design a Tracking System

Design some kind of system that will let you know where you have sent applications and on what date. The system can fit whatever kind of search you are involved in, but should permit you to be an informed responder if and when someone calls you. You do not want to be in the position a candidate was in with me several years ago when I made a phone call to determine if the candidate was still interested in our position, and, if so, could we discuss a campus visit and arrangements for some background checks with people who were listed on the application as well as others in his place of employment. When he responded to my initial phone contact with questions about who I was, where I was calling from, which institution that was, what was the position I was referencing, what was the location of the institution, quite a bit became clear about his level of specific interest in the job we had open. The problem was magnified by the fact that the materials in his application had indicated that he was not applying to other institutions, because what we described in the announcements which had been printed in professional listings had been "exactly what he was seeking."

If he had been invited to campus and if he had been interviewed, I do not know if he would have been offered a position or not. I do know that he certainly reduced his chance of being considered because he had obviously sent out so many applications—"blanketing the market"—that he had lost track and thus became much less attractive to us as potential employers.

Another important piece of a tracking system is a record of when positions close. If you do not hear from an institution, is it acceptable to ask where they are in the application process? Yes, but if you call to inquire 2 weeks before the position closes, it does not look good to the institution. Including a date of closing also lets you know when you might expect to hear from someone and gives you an indication of when it is reasonable to inquire about the status of your application.

Know the Law

As a student, a job applicant, or an employer, it is important to know what legal implications exist for people and institutions related to employment. Any large organization will have persons in the personnel or human resources departments who can inform you about employment law, what you can and cannot be asked, how open your records are, and what can happen during the application and screening process.

Persons who have worked in large institutions for several years may be able to tell stories about things that happened during job interviews, which were direct violations of employment law or human service policies. I once worked with a woman who would routinely ask female candidates, "What does your husband do and can he support you?" Each time, I would call a halt to the interview and explain that the question was inappropriate and did not need to be answered. In nearly every case, the female interviewee would respond, "That's OK, I'll be glad to answer that." Other, more invasive questions—whether illegal or just inappropriate based on common courtesy—included questions to female applicants about whether they planned to have children; to male candidates I have heard questions about how much they planned to be at home and do child care. Other similar questions I would just as soon forget. Most of the inappropriate questions fall into the "I'm-curious-and-want-to-know" category.

Though laws have changed and there is more emphasis on training interviewers on what is appropriate and what is not, breeches of etiquette or law still happen. Applicants would be well advised to check the laws. An additional good practice would be to discuss some of the inappropriate questions one might be asked and rehearse possible responses with colleagues.

Current employment law and hiring practice have also changed what most recommending institutions can and cannot do with respect to providing background information when requested. In former days, huge amounts of personal information might be shared by reference sources with potential employers—either through letter, by phone, or through personal contact. Many employers today have adopted personnel practices that limit what they say about former employees to confirmation of prior employment, position title, and inclusive dates of employment. Although this may conform to the letter of the law, it does not advantage a candidate because the recommending institution does not go ahead and describe positive characteristics, effective work skills, strengths of character, and positive rankings on performance evaluation. Of course, the institution also does not pass along misconceptions, bad perceptions, biased supervisor evaluations, or unfounded rumor. The system has both advantages and disadvantages.

A FINAL NOTE

I once again recommend informational interviews as a means of preparing yourself for employment. A second benefit is to prepare a potential employer for you as a possible applicant. If you have completed an information interview with someone where you later are an applicant for a position, it may provide that edge that lets the institution take notice of your résumé and application in a pile of others, resulting in an invitation to interview. The rest is up to you.

IV

This section provides the reader with a more focused discussion of licensing and certification issues, even though they have been mentioned several times throughout the chapters so far. It also provides the reader with a look at 14 people who moved on from their original counseling positions to other related fields.

Chapter 12, "Certification and Licensing," repeats some of the information that has been scattered through previous chapters; however, in this chapter, there is more of a focus on the broad concepts of certification and licensing. The reader needs to be informed about which licenses apply for the particular counseling position he or she hopes to have in the future. Licensing particulars will also influence the preparation program a person chooses to enter, and they will influence the courses a person takes during that preparation program.

There is a heavy emphasis throughout this chapter, and in the rest of the book, on readers taking responsibility for their own check-off procedures with respect to preparation programs, licensing requirements, job search strategies, and background preparation. They should know what the requirements are for each step along the way to their chosen professional position.

Chapter 13, "Profiles," is made up of 14 different stories. I interviewed 14 people who initially received preparation as counselors. The career journey for each one is briefly presented with stories about how they made decisions to move on to other positions. In the words of one of the interviewees, "Counselor education was good preparation for work I never thought that I'd do." Another person profiled said she wished she would have known during the counselor preparation program that the preparation would open other doors.

I encourage you, the reader, to look for the consistent themes across each of the 14 profiles. As the interviewer, I was struck by the common stories I heard from each person interviewed. In fact, I began to wonder if I was planting suggestions with them because some of the themes emerged so frequently. After listening again to interview tapes, I decided that the themes were emerging spontaneously. Throughout this book I strongly encourage readers to develop their own interviews and their own data collection processes.

Chapter 14—"Have You Found Your Way?"—returns to the issue raised in the opening chapter of this book, "Finding Your Way." Only the reader can answer that one. I hope this book has given you some opportunity to address the question.

A final section, an Appendix, lists a number of professional associations that serve persons in the counseling professions. I am not including addresses, for they can change over time. I am also not including telephone numbers for the same reason. And, finally, I am not including Web or Internet addresses because I know the modern reader can quickly find those if he or she starts with the name of the professional association. I am aware that professional association names change as the organizations adjust to different populations, to different member needs, to mergers and organizational changes, and to changes in other regulations. I trust that if that happens, the modern reader will be able to track down the newly named organization with one or two mouse clicks.

Enjoy.

12

CERTIFICATION AND LICENSING

Some counseling specialties require a license for persons who intend to practice that specialty. Others call for a certificate. Some counseling professional practices do not require either a license or a certificate. You need to be sure you know what applies to the specialty you selected for yourself.

Licenses are issued by state agencies, and the requirements may differ from state to state. Certificates are usually granted by an accrediting agency; however, in some states, the state issues certificates for counseling specialties.

The word *license* is sometimes a part of the title of a person in a particular specialty: Licensed Clinical Social Worker, Licensed Psychologist. The word *certificate* might be used in other counseling specialties: Certified Clinical Mental Health Counselor, Certified Substance Abuse Counselor.

Other counseling specialties may use a descriptor without either of the words *license* or *certified* as part of the title: Marriage and Family Therapist, Substance Abuse Counselor, School Counselor, School Psychologist, Counselor.

The difference between a license and a certificate can be confusing. In general, a license means that the person who holds the license is the only one authorized to do what the license calls for. Often, a certificate means that a person who holds a certificate has completed certain preparation programs or has met certain criteria attached to the function of the position associated with the certificate. Being certified does not always mean that you are the only person who can perform certain professional tasks.

For example, a counselor and a certified counselor can do the same things in terms of their professional practice. If a state requires psychologists to be licensed, then a person without a psychologist license cannot perform the functions of a psychologist. In licensing categories, there are nearly always lists of functions that may or may not be performed by people holding that license.

The best way for you to determine what applies to the specialty of your choice is to study the regulations in the state or states where you plan to work. Information about certification and counseling is available on the Web site of every state and can usually be obtained with a few simple search strategies.

Using the Web browser of your computer, search on a combination of terms that includes the name of the counseling specialty of your interest (for example, marriage and family therapy) plus the words *license* or *certificate* and the name of the state. Do a second search changing the word *license* to the word *certificate*. If you think you might live in a different state at some time, conduct additional searches, putting in the names of the states that are probable places for you. To expand your knowledge of various counseling specialties, repeat your Web searching with other counselor specialties included in your combination of terms: school counselor, psychologist, social worker, mental health counselor, mental health therapist, rehabilitation counselor, or other specialties you know that can give you a more complete picture of career opportunities in counseling.

Once you have become more certain about the counseling specialty you prefer, use your Web browser for additional searches: add the word *jobs* to your title search and see what information you obtain. Use other terms—*employment, statistics, income, educational programs*—and see what you get.

An additional source of information for you to consider in your examination of certification and licensing are the classified ads in the Yellow Pages of your phone book. See how many listings there are for counseling positions that include the word *certified* or *licensed* in the listing. Make a note of the kind of license or certificate mentioned and return to your Web search to see if those descriptions are any different than the ones you previously searched. If the differences are not clear, then feel free to contact the person who posts that particular certificate or license in his or her advertisement and ask that person about his or her credentialing.

You must be cautious about licenses and certificates for any specialty area. It is possible to create an organization that issues licenses or certificates with fancy sounding names attached to specialty areas of all kinds. Just because a group says you can be certified in their specialty does not mean that the certificate or license is a valid credential that enables you to practice a counseling specialty for financial gain.

One test for the validity of counseling specialty licenses and credentials is to obtain information from agencies that employ counselors and from the agencies or organizations that pay counselors. For example, ask the personnel office of a school district about the certificates or licenses they require before they hire a school counselor, a school social worker, a school psychologist, or other counseling specialist who might work in the schools. Do the same thing for other employing agencies—hospitals, county mental health agencies, rehabilitation centers, and the like.

One final check you might make is with several insurance companies. Ask them which licenses or certificates are required for them to approve funding for services provided by persons with particular counseling specialties.

13

PROFILES

Counselor education was the best preparation for a job I never thought I'd have.

Tom Eversole

This chapter contains brief profiles of 14 people who began their professional careers in one of the counseling fields. They have each moved on to a different position, but each continues to use the basic counseling skills and the knowledge base they valued as part of their initial preparation.

I interviewed each of the 14 people, using a very broad, open-ended interview format. I had a few questions that I used with each person, but I did not use a rigid question and answer format.

Included in each interview were questions asking about their present job and a few questions to determine the path from their initial counseling position to the position they currently hold. I asked what was involved in their initial decision to enter a preparation program for counseling, and I asked each person what were the satisfactions and the dissatisfactions or stressors in their work. Finally, I asked each person what were the core counseling skills from their initial preparation which they continue to use in their present work. In a few cases, I asked if the person had plans beyond his or her current job.

Each of the people interviewed was known to me. Six of the people were former students—one in high school and five in graduate school. Five of the people I had met through my professional association—the American Counseling Association. Three of the people I had met or worked with through community projects or consulting relationships.

Two of the interviews were conducted by telephone; the rest were completed in face-to-face meetings.

Following the interview, I prepared a brief profile, trying to hold each profile to about a thousand words. I then sent a copy of the profile to the person asking him or her to edit or correct for accuracy and completeness. Each person returned the edited copy to me electronically, and I made additional edits before sending a hard copy for the person's approval to use in this book. Each person gave approval for me to use his or her name and to use the name of institutions or places mentioned in the interviews.

Conducting these interviews was very enjoyable, and I recommend that readers do the same (as I have repeatedly mentioned throughout this book). My pleasure was not just reconnecting with people I have known over the years. My pleasure came from learning from people who were doing interesting things that they enjoyed. It was intriguing to hear people describe their career paths and to have them comment on the dips, twists, and turns that carried them from some starting point in the past to the place they are today.

None of the 14 people would have predicted where they are today if they had been asked at the start of their undergraduate or even their graduate careers. A few of the people said that if they had been asked about their current position when they were starting out, they would have laughed or would have insisted they would not be in such a place.

I was struck by some similarities among the 14 interviewees. The word *passion* came up in repeated interviews. I listened to several of my tape recordings a second time to see if I was suggesting the word in the interviews—I did not. *Passion* or *passionate* came up spontaneously in conversations. People said, "I'm passionate about children's issues," or, "I have a passion for seeing that families have better lives." One person used the word *calling* to describe her work, saying, "I have a calling to do what I'm doing."

A second consistent theme among the 14 interviewees was the numerous descriptions of how the persons saw their jobs as enabling them to do something significant for other people. That theme was expanded by several who described moves from one job situation to another because they would be able to have more influence on the lives of persons in a different professional position. For example, becoming a school administrator would let a person have an impact on more students than they would have seen as a counselor. Or, becoming a teacher of counselors or becoming the director of a policy institute would let them have a positive impact on more than they could reach as a counselor working one at a time.

A strong commitment to social responsibility emerges from many of the 14 interviews. Perhaps no one expressed it more strongly than Todd Noble, who explained that there had been a strong push in his graduate program to avoid private practice and to work, instead, in organizations designed to be more socially responsible.

Some of the 14 interviewees are approaching retirement. A few are in the early stages of their careers. Those who are near retirement say they could not have predicted where they ended up if they had been asked early in their careers. Those in the early years of their careers are not sure where their career path will take them.

I hope, as you read these profiles, that you will be able to identify with some of the issues described by each person. I am also hopeful that you will decide to do your own interviews as another means of looking at your own life and trying to decide if one of the counseling professions is really for you.

BREE HAYES

Bree Hayes is President of The Hayes Group, a virtual company—she has 40 associates who work for the firm, but there is no physical office building. The associates include persons from counseling psychology, clinical psychology, business management, and an employment attorney. Bree's route to her current position has taken a number of interesting turns.

As an undergraduate, Bree was preparing to be a public school teacher. Early on, she knew that she was more fascinated by the ways that students interact and by how they learn than by the content of their learning.

As a graduate student in both her master's and doctoral work, Bree initially thought that she would have a career in counseling—private practice or as a professor. She also discovered that she had more interest in group work than in one-on-one processes and says that she took every opportunity to study group dynamics that she could find. "I took group courses in psych, social work, counseling, and business," she said during our interview. Bree also joked that she thinks her Counseling Psych doctorate at Boston University may have been the longest on record.

During her doctoral work, Bree had a job with a community mental health agency as Director of Consultation and Education. "As a part of the Comprehensive Community Mental Health Act, our program was tasked with community outreach, including wellness programs." While in that position, she wrote a grant for an employee assistance program (EAP). Major companies already had EAPs, and Bree began to make presentations for smaller companies on issues of stress, substance abuse, wellness, addictions, and financial problems—very broad-based mental health issues.

At one of the presentations, a woman told Bree that she would like to have her husband's company have the kind of presentation in which she had just participated. Her husband worked for IBM. Bree did a presentation for the local office, and an IBM executive from a different region was present who arranged for her to expand her work. That began Bree's work with large and small companies.

She laughs about the days of the breakthrough to business and industry, saying that she talked with a friend and explained, "I don't know anything about business; I'm a counselor." He advised her to work on her vocabulary: "Don't say 'share your experience,' say, 'let's process the dynamics of this interaction.'" The presentations for IBM began to expand, and Bree continued to do stress management and conflict management sessions for a year throughout the Midwest.

Bree then left the community mental health center and formed a company, Resource Management Services (RMS), in concert with two other employees from the mental health center. RMS expanded rapidly and created offices in 13 states where client businesses had their own facilities.

When Bree's spouse took a job at the University of Georgia, she sold her portion of the company to her partners and taught for a couple of years, but, in time, wanted to return to consulting. "I missed my life on the road," she said, and explained that, "I really felt like I had a calling." Bree explains that when working with people in business, she felt she was teaching them critically important knowledge and skill sets that let them be more effective in their work. Bree went back to the consulting world by taking a job with RHR International—"the oldest organizational consulting company around; the granddaddies of it all," she said.

Bree worked for RHR for 7 years, with her typical routine being to get on a plane on Sunday evening and get home on Friday, visiting a different city each day. "I loved what I was doing, but in time, it wore me out. Consulting companies typically take two-thirds of every dollar you earn—I earned a lot of money for them but I learned a lot about the business: how to write a proposal, how to market, and how to bill." Bree took that knowledge to her current position as President of The Hayes Group. "I still work a very very full week, but I am not on the road every day and that is good. I keep two major clients for whom I do most of the work and they keep me as busy as I want."

One project The Hayes Group offers to a large power company is a comprehensive developmental program for their promising managers. Advanced Management Program (AMP) includes a 360 assessment, an intensive week of management instruction, and the creation of a development plan. Additionally, a coach is assigned to each participant, with regular coaching contacts and assignments. Bree says that she does fewer of the presentations herself because she uses experts in each subject area. "I sit in the back of the room a lot," she said. She also does executive assessments for some of the companies, examining persons who are prospective hires, working with managers who are failing and need some coaching, and helping to develop those people who are being groomed for a more senior position.

I asked Bree to reflect on the skill set that she uses today, which she acquired in her original counselor preparation. She immediately said, "Family systems—it's there all the time." She explained that situations like corporate mergers are prime examples of instances where a study of family dynamics or family systems has direct applicability to what happens with employees in a merger. "It's like a new child wanting the older child's toys and they don't want to give them up; or, it's like who gets Daddy's attention."

Bree says her understanding of human development is crucial. "I continuously use the communication skills I learned in grad school, but now I find myself teaching others those same skills. Many of the executives with whom I work have listening problems." She adds process observation and group skills to the list. "I use different styles for different clients. For example, I might text younger clients, but make phone calls to older clients."

Bree gets the greatest satisfaction from doing something in a company that takes the company to new heights and thinking, "I had something to do with that." She points out, "I've made hard calls also—even suggesting strongly that a person needed to be terminated and then seeing that the replacement person helped the company take off and be successful. It's not all mine, but I may have had a little bit to do with that."

When I asked about the sources of dissatisfaction, she said, "My mind and body are out of sync. When I was 40, I didn't have the experience or expertise to do what I now do. At this age, I have the experience, but wish I had a younger body to go along with this frenetic lifestyle. I don't know how to relax. Working this hard has an impact on how you live all of your life. You have to be mentally and physically in shape at all times."

Bree ended our interview by saying, "I love my life. I'm not complaining. You have to be willing to put on your sneakers at the airport and run from one appointment to another. I like that every day is different, but I am aware that it is a demanding career. I tell my coaching clients they can call me at any hour—and some of them do. They call because they are used to instant responses and they frequently forget that I'm on central time zone."

"I'm very happy with how my career turned out"

CHRISTIE PLINSKI

Many school counselors continue on an education career path to school administration. One example is Christie Plinski, who started her career as a secondary school teacher, then stopped when her children were young but stayed connected to active school involvement by serving 3 years as an elected member of the school board in a small community. Then, as a single parent, she made the move to graduate school in counseling. Christie completed a master's degree in counseling and worked as an elementary school counselor in a rural school with high poverty rates and identified drug problems. She also worked as a school counselor in a large suburban high school and in a medium-sized senior high school before obtaining her administrator certificate. She worked in subsequent jobs as an assistant principal and then as a principal of a technical high school in a large urban city. She points out that the job of school counselor was very different in each of the schools.

Christie said, "There's not a day goes by that, as a principal, I didn't use the skills I learned in my counseling program—listening, caring, and group process—whether it's in a staff meeting, or working with an upset teacher, student, or parent." The choice to become a counselor came after considering and rejecting other career professions—including law school. Christie had even taken the Law School Admission Test (LSAT) as an undergraduate student but rejected that path because of time and expense. She did not think it would provide the kind of "people focus" she knew she wanted as a young college student. A teacher education program seemed the best avenue for her, and even as a student teacher, she asked to watch the school counselor at work, interested in what that profession would provide. In her words, she said that she knew nothing about school counseling—even thinking, at the time, that it was something like what a psychiatrist would do.

Christie has always been a high achiever: "I never knew how to study for a 'B' and I was always focused." In graduate school, Christie's fellow students and the faculty saw her as focused, achievement oriented, and able to handle multiple tasks simultaneously—characteristics that have served her well as counselor and as school administrator.

The driving focus for Christie in all her career decisions has been the students she served. She explained that she has always wanted to see students "connected" and able to make good choices that serve them well in later life. When she worked as a school counselor, she pointed out that she was able "to use both my head and my heart." For Christie, "counseling was like a rebirth for me." Her school counseling positions have all been the most satisfying for her professionally.

The move to school administration was influenced by two major factors: "As a single parent, I needed more income to support a family; and, I saw school administration as a place where I could have an increased impact on what kids need." The career change was also a part of Christie's characteristic quest "to keep moving, to learn more, to have a greater impact." That quest continues at present, as Christie, now in her 50s, retires from school administration and enters graduate school again to pursue doctoral study. "Teaching and consulting are in my future," she says.

"The school counseling graduate program and my school counseling experience gave me a lot of content which I used daily as a school administrator," Christie said. "Knowledge about special education, student staffing procedures, service and program availability, and the variety of social services which can be accessed for students was something I used frequently as a school principal." She also explained how her counseling knowledge came in to play by being able to make informal assessments of student behaviors and deciding when to vigorously pursue referrals. Christie described one instance in which she saw the early signs of a psychotic break and was able to go with a student and parents to an emergency treatment program where the student did receive help—"The student was able to return to school later and did graduate on schedule."

Caring a great deal about students and educational programs can be frustrating for both school counselors and school administrators if school districts or other teachers are not supportive or cooperative in reaching those same goals. Both as a school counselor and as a school administrator, Christie said she has seen counselors who had entered the profession for "the wrong reasons." She expressed concern about counselors who are unaware of national standards for their profession or who do not continue to pursue knowledge and skill to be used to benefit students.

Christie explained that both counselors and principals must be able to deal with conflict and stress. She has experienced both—as a young school board member in a community where there was a teacher strike, she received threatening phone calls, had the tires slashed on her car, and had her children's teachers flash inappropriate signs to her. As a counselor, she would not be silent when she needed to speak up on behalf of students. As a school principal, she found herself in hot water when she worked to document inappropriate teacher behavior and to change school district policies that she saw as not supportive of students.

School administration can be physically stressful as well, as Christie can attest having taken a stress leave from her work after conflict over district-level policy changes. In addition, she suffered a back injury while trying to break up a fight among a large group of students in front of the school following a homecoming dance. "I really felt alone; here I was, with other administrators, in the middle of a gang fight, when six police cars were parked across the street just watching what was going on." Christie continues to talk about her years as a counselor and administrator with positive feelings. She repeatedly describes how good it feels to be supported in her actions and decisions by teachers—several of whom were quoted in newspaper articles about her saying she was the best principal they had ever worked with and that she was supportive of teachers and an advocate for kids.

As a counselor and as a school principal, Christie said that contact with individuals—students, teachers, parents—was the most satisfying part of her jobs. Building trust and relationships required use of her counseling skills in both positions. "When I could see a trusting relationship lead to effective decisions that a person would make, that gave me a lot of pleasure," she said. As a school principal, Christie explained that working with teachers to develop goals, plans for the future, and vision for education was tremendously satisfying.

The disappointing parts of being a principal relate to the same dimension of her work—to see a faculty work hard to develop vision, goals, and plans only to have them not be supported by other school administrators produced a lot of dissatisfaction on Christie's part. "When there is no support for your work, it hurts, whether you are a student, a teacher, or a school administrator."

The parts of the school counseling job which were less satisfying for Christie were tasks she labels as "tedium"—checking schedules and credits, enrollment, seemingly endless paperwork. Christie describes herself as very organized, so she managed the tedious tasks quickly and used the opportunities to have good quality contact with students. She also expressed disappointment in other counselors who did not use the necessary paperwork contacts with students as chances to improve relationships.

The next step in Christie's professional career will be a doctoral program in educational leadership followed by university teaching and work as a consultant with school administrators. Her counseling skills will again be put to good use as she will be supervising student teachers as a graduate student job while she works on her own courses. "It's all about trust and relationships," she said.

EVELYN ALLEN

Evelyn Allen began her professional life as a high school teacher. "I didn't like it," she said. "There wasn't any way that I could do everything I needed to do for as many students as had needs when I had such big classes. It was not satisfying." She is winding down her career as an attorney working as a child advocate in the court system—"very satisfying work—I can see things happening because of what I do." As Evelyn lets go of some of her child advocacy work and hands that off to other attorneys, she continues to use her counseling training with senior citizens and families. "Counseling training helped me to ask the questions people don't think they want to talk about. Counseling training is good for helping people think—to help them look at other options."

Evelyn enrolled in graduate school in counseling, seeing it as one way that she could become more effective with a few students rather than be ineffective (in her words) with many. When she graduated, she worked as a high school counselor for a while and found that satisfying. "I could have some individual time with students and felt that I was being helpful with a lot of things—career decisions, academic preparation, family crises, personal stuff."

Having grown up on a farm and valuing small-town and rural life, Evelyn and her husband looked for positions that would meet those criteria. "Finding a school counseling position in rural Kansas was difficult—there aren't that many positions to begin with and when one does open, there are a lot of applicants and the people who get hired tend to remain in those positions forever." She was investing a lot of her energy in raising her own children, but found a way to enroll in law school.

In our interview, Evelyn said that she did not have an idealized picture of what a law practice would be like, but she knew that she wanted to remain in rural Kansas and be able to parent her children as well as be in the same locale as her husband. Evelyn's husband had made the move from public school teaching to banking, and it looked like they had found a permanent location for their family and work.

"I would have liked to have continued as a school counselor, it was satisfying, but the options weren't available. That's when I moved into the practice of law."

Evelyn was at the early edge of women's entry to the practice of law: she was one of only a few female law students and even fewer practicing attorneys. "It was great when I'd go to a meeting or to a continuing education event—there was never a line at the bathroom." She also said that it was a bit lonely.

"I never wanted to be a trial attorney," Evelyn said. "I'd be assigned by the court to provide legal defense services for an accused person and I had problems with that—at times, I knew they were guilty but I needed to provide a good legal defense. That went against much of what I was raised to do and be."

Evelyn worked as an assistant district attorney in a rural county and enjoyed part of that work. She finally found her niche, however, when she was asked by a judge to serve as a child advocate in one case. That experience grew and she continued to spend the bulk of her time in the practice of law as a child and family advocate—working in and with the courts to see that the best things possible would happen for the children who came through the court system. "That was very satisfying," she said.

Evelyn describes herself as a very practical person. "I felt best when I knew that because of what I was doing that a child's life might be improved or that a family situation might be better." She went ahead to explain, "Things didn't always turn out the way I would have liked them to be, but if the final result was better than at the start, I could accept that."

I asked Evelyn what counseling skills she took in to child advocacy legal work. She answered, "I think I could really listen to what kids were saying—not just the words, but the emotions and feelings and experiences. Sometimes, it wasn't even in what they specifically said as much as in what I understood them to be saying between the lines that let me work more effectively with them, the courts, their families, and the agencies that served them." She added, "Over the life of a case, I would often be the one person in the child's life who remained constant—social workers changed, judges changed, others changed, but I'd be the constant."

Evelyn would regularly take pictures of the children she worked with and present the photos to them as one more way to help them feel good about themselves. The photos helped Evelyn stay connected with child clients over the sometimes several years of a continuing case.

I asked Evelyn if there had been a time as a high school student or when she was in college if she had thought about a different career path or if people had suggested other professional possibilities. She thought for a minute about that and stated that if law school had been mentioned when she was a high school student that she would probably have laughed that one off. She had thought about some kind of office work in personnel or management, but had rejected that, in part, because it would mean being in a large city and the pull of small-town and rural life was so strong that it pushed such career options out of consideration.

"I really liked going to school; I liked writing; I liked study; I was good at that—teaching emerged, but even during my student teaching experience, it was just so stressful that I knew I could never do this and be good enough at it for it to be a life-long career." Today, Evelyn still carries a few child advocate cases. She has handed off some of the cases that required her to drive long distances in order to do the work. And she has "graduated" some of the cases she has carried for a long time, because the children have reached the age at which they no longer qualify for child court supervision.

I asked about the most distressing parts of her career. She answered, "Some judges don't listen." When I asked if it was that they did not listen or if they did not listen to women, she smiled, and said, "Both."

"Counseling was good preparation for the legal part of my career."

HOWARD SMITH

Howard Smith is the Interim Dean of the College of Education and Counseling at South Dakota State University (SDSU). Howard's career began in a far different place—he was a young clergyman serving a rather conservative Protestant church in a conservative community. Neither the church nor the community leaders were very pleased when Howard became quite public with his thinking when he participated in antiwar parades during the Vietnam era. He made other public statements in meetings and from the pulpit on controversial issues which were not well received. That characteristic is probably observed throughout Howard's career, because he speaks passionately about people and human issues and he speaks what he believes is right. At the time, it brought a rather quick end to his pastoral career, but it has not dampened his commitment or his action. He acknowledges that he works more effectively now—"I don't let my passions carry me away in a conversation. When that happens, I lose."

Howard moved to Kansas City and began work with a regional human rights commission. It gave him an opportunity to work with people in a different manner and on a different level than he had in the ministry. The experience solidified Howard's realization that he needed a career in which he could work with people and be able to have an impact on their life conditions. That led to a second graduate degree, and he added a master's in counseling to his master's degree in divinity. He also realized that he could not stop with the master's degrees and obtained an Ed.D. while working in a private mental health practice.

Howard's next career move was to counselor education at SDSU and then to department head. Although his work setting was changing, much of his focus on improving the lives of people remained and actually became more instrumental. Howard said that he realized that if he spent his entire career in private practice working with people in a one-on-one situation that he could have a positive impact on a lot of people over a career lifetime; however, "If I could influence even one piece of legislation, I realized that I could have an impact on hundreds or even thousands of individuals."

The interest in legislation and public policy turned into a course requirement in his teaching. During each legislative session, students were to track bills in the state legislature and do analyses of their effect on people. Howard speaks about those class activities with a lot of enthusiasm and good feeling about what students were able to do as part of their regular class activities. "One year, 65% of the bills introduced in the state legislature had something to do with people or education."

Howard's wife, Kris, was pursuing her own graduate degree program, and the two of them had serious discussions about being a dual-career couple. The possibility existed that they might not find employment in the same community or in the same institution, and the discussions included possibilities of being both a dual-career and a dual-location couple.

Instead of Howard or Kris finding a position where the other would follow, they both received nearly simultaneous job offers in two different locations. Their decision was to accept both positions for a period they agreed not to exceed 5 years. That was 16 years ago. They have both changed positions since that original decision, but their career changes have not taken them to a common location.

Howard was one of the founding members of the American Mental Health Counseling Association and was elected president during the formative years of that professional group. That experience gave him an inside look at professional association activities, and he developed an appreciation for how professional associations can have a positive influence on both the members and the larger community. He used that knowledge and experience to apply for and obtain a position with the American Counseling Association (ACA) as Associate Executive Director for Professional Affairs—a position he held for 5 years and which put Kris and him in closer proximity while she was working on the east coast.

Through his work with ACA, Howard was able to be closely involved with federal legislation. He also developed some of the early relationships and protocols for members of ACA to be involved with the American Red Cross disaster relief operations. He describes that as an opportunity for him to continue to be involved in client service, but it also fits with his broader orientation to helping—if he could train or facilitate the work of others, then it multiplied the effect he could have if he were to be a sole provider. In his Red Cross work, his legislative work, his oversight of convention program content, and in other activities, Howard was able to live out his passions and feel good about the effect he had on benefit for others. At the same time, he says that he missed higher education and the kind of interaction he had with students.

Howard returned to SDSU where he currently serves as dean in the interim. When I asked Howard how he liked higher education administration, he told me, "I miss the helping relationships I had with clients and with students. That's one of the reasons I continue my work with Red Cross disaster services—it's a place where I can personally do some work and can be influential in seeing that others provide services to people in critical situations, like post-Katrina." Howard said that there are satisfactions in administration. "I like it when I can call a faculty member in and tell them, 'That was a great thing that you did.'" He also likes being able to help new faculty get a foothold in their professional work. It was not surprising that Howard said his biggest frustration being a dean is some of the personnel work that goes along with the job.

"I'm using my counseling skills daily," he said. "Whether it's listening to a faculty member who is having some kind of problem or working with a student who is stressed out. I see myself as trying to increase a person's ability to respond—*response-ability,* I call it." And always, there is the opportunity as dean for Howard to realize his passion—making things better for people in as many ways as he can.

KRIS SMITH

Kris Smith is Associate Provost for Institutional Research at George Mason University in Fairfax, Virginia. It's a long way from the "ideal job" she identified early in her career—half-time home economics teacher and half-time school counselor. Kris had begun her career in education teaching home economics in a South Dakota high school. She felt she had a pretty good understanding of people—growing up, she had been a good observer of her own difficult family dynamics and had developed numerous effective coping strategies in her life. Kris developed a need "to help people—to save the world almost." She saw school counseling as a place where she could extend her eagerness to help others, but the idea of returning to graduate school seemed out of the realm of possibility at the time.

Following her mother's death, Kris's younger sister asked her, "If you could do anything in the world you want to do, what would it be?" Kris's immediate response was to "return to graduate school," which her sister urged her to do as the way their mother would have wanted them to use the small inheritance that had come their way.

Kris even considered developing a specialty in addictions counseling, following on her experience in Al-Anon as a teen. She decided that "it would be too confining, too close to my own experience," and that she could find other arenas where she could help people.

In graduate school, Kris had a part-time job in the university counseling center. She also organized the operation of the campus crisis hotline—probably not the first time and certainly not the last time that her organizational and management skills were noted and utilized by others. Her interest in being a high school counselor and home economics teacher began to shift toward work with students in higher education.

Kris used her new degree in counseling in other ways. She worked with her husband, Howard Smith, in doing some consulting with businesses. Kris worked with persons in the Human Resources department and found that her knowledge of family systems and her counseling skills were put to good use.

It did not take long for Kris to decide that she could do more good for more people with an advanced degree. She began looking for graduate schools where she could combine studies in student services and research. Her systematic search for the right school was influenced by the fact that she and Howard needed to work out a relationship that would involve periods of separation, as each had a career with occupational tugs and pulls that did not always carry them in the same direction. The picture of a dual-career–dual-location couple which emerges is worth study. Kris and Howard had long discussions about ideal jobs, ideal location, and the way they would manage both if they were not in the same institution or the same city.

Kris had nearly settled on a doctoral institution for her next phase of graduate study when a chance meeting with a person at an ACA convention resulted in a question about why she was not considering a different institution. The conversation developed into an additional application for graduate study and admission to a doctoral program. Kris's self-confidence combined with her negotiating skills came in to play when the university gave her an offer of employment as a graduate student and a time line for her graduate work. She responded to request a different time schedule and different employment conditions—which were accepted. This action seems characteristic of Kris, who is not afraid to state what she needs and to work to get it.

When Kris finished her doctoral degree, she and Howard had another of those necessary discussions in a dual-career–dual-location marriage. The discussion resulted in a decision that the two of them would begin job searches and whoever got the best offer, the other would follow to that place. The complication arose when they simultaneously received equivalent job offers in different locations. They revised their plans and each accepted new jobs—a situation that once again required a long-distance marriage.

As Kris has moved from one job to the next, she has always looked to the new with eagerness. "I love creating new things," she said, and new positions have always meant new challenges and opportunities to develop programs, improve the way things function, and deliver services to students. In her present job, Kris says, "I love telling the story about how good institutional research can do so much for students. Many people think of this as a dry or dull kind of job, but I can look at major programs which have been implemented which our research program has helped influence. I love being able to do things for students."

I asked Kris about continued use of the counseling skills she acquired in her first graduate degree, and she answered, "I use my counseling skills every day—it's a matter of listening, hearing, and encouraging people to help them do what they want to do." She added, "My counseling skills are important when it comes to dealing with difficult employees, dealing with administrators and faculty." With a little tone of regret, Kris said, "I do think my counseling skills have lost a little edge." In her daily work, Kris says she has a lot of support from administrators and points out that one reason she was hired was because of her counseling background.

Personnel issues cause Kris the most stress in her current job, and the ability to see that she is having a positive impact on a large number of students is one of her greatest rewards. "I grew up with some strong messages from my mother—being of service to others is one; and seeing people as equal is another. In my current job, I can help level the playing field for others." The strong need to be of service is projected into Kris's future when she talks about potential retirement as an opportunity to become more intensely involved in volunteer service activities of some kind.

We ended our conversation with Kris saying, "I get feedback from students that tells me I'm having an impact. I enjoy telling the story of what an office like mine can do. And I'm excited about what other things I can create from this office which will have positive benefits for other people. I'm not done yet."

JULIE KNUTSON

"I wish that during my undergraduate and graduate programs I would have heard that preparation in counseling or counseling psychology opens the door to other possibilities, not just counseling or therapy." Julie Knutson made that statement near the end of our interview in response to my question: "What would you have liked to have known early on in your career that you know now?"

Julie is the President and Chief Executive Officer (CEO) of the Oklahoma Academy for State Goals. The Oklahoma Academy is a private, nonprofit membership organization that identifies the critical public policy issues facing Oklahoma's future. The Academy's mission is to identify issues facing Oklahoma; provide well-researched, objective information; foster nonpartisan collaboration; develop responsible recommendations; and encourage community and legislative action (www.okacademy.org).

Julie moved to the Oklahoma Academy from her job as a school counselor and secondary school vice principal in 1987. She says she became a school counselor in order to provide a better way for students to be heard and have a voice in their own choices. Much of what she currently does in her work with the Academy carries out the same goal.

In her first teaching and counseling job, Julie says she wanted to be someone in the school system who would help students explore career opportunities and to help teachers, parents, and students talk with each other more effectively. There was also a desire to work on behalf of students who were experiencing some of the more stressful aspects of growing up—students with fears and concerns who needed an advocate in the system to improve communication with parents, teachers, and peers.

People who know Julie describe her as organized, task oriented, focused on accomplishing goals, and very effective in bringing different groups together for dialogue in pursuit of mutual goals. She has also been described as one who sees "the big picture" and who is passionate about her work.

Julie's introduction to the Academy came when she attended a conference they sponsored. As a school counselor, she had asked the superintendent of schools to pay for her attendance at the conference where Oklahoma's future was the topic of discussion. Julie was concerned about finding ways to help students, parents, and schools see that education and the state's economic future were inextricably linked and thought that the topic announced for the conference fit her needs.

"At the close of the conference, I got in a conversation with some of the Academy board members and shared some of my ideas about education and Oklahoma's future. Sometime after that, I was invited to submit an application for the position of Executive Director." With some hesitance on her part to even apply, Julie made it through the search process, which included a pool of 250 applicants and three finalists. After she was hired, she asked what brought her to be the candidate of choice and heard two answers: "Your positive outlook and your counseling and psychology background."

I asked Julie what skills she brought to the administrative position with the Academy which were similar to the skills she practiced as a school counselor. She told me that she was a good listener—"not just hearing what people say, but what they were really meaning and feeling." She also said that people seemed to feel comfortable with her and that it was easy to develop trust relationships—"even when we disagree." Julie said that, "I have a collaborative style—it's important to be able to work together."

The listening, communication, and collaborative skills serve her well as president and CEO of the Academy. She has a board of directors made up of 79 members and an executive committee of 33 people—all of whom are prominent persons in the private sector, in education, and government. "They come to the table with different agendas and ideas and I work with them so that we can move ahead with projects that benefit the whole state."

Developing new projects and creating new programs was common when Julie worked as a school counselor. As a middle school counselor, she developed a proposal to involve parents more in student enrollment and career decision making. She got administrators to support that idea and saw that it was implemented. As a high school counselor, she was tagged to be the director of guidance and worked to implement a plan where vice principals and counselors were paired with an identified group of students. The ability to see the big picture, to develop plans to reach goals, and to organize people in pursuit of common goals continues to be a requisite skill in her role with the Academy.

I asked Julie what was different about working in school systems or with the Academy, and she quickly responded that the Academy is made up of powerful decision makers who do not hesitate to take risks, make decisions, and argue for their point. "In education, decision making and change take longer," Julie said. "The ideas may be just as good, but the picture is usually a little smaller. Academy members are thinking about the state of Oklahoma and beyond rather than a school or a school district. Both groups are exciting to work with."

Stepping into a new field, like she did when she took the Academy job, had its anxieties. "Frankly, I was scared—could I do this?" Julie explained that her mother had always been a factor in her approach to jobs—"You can do anything if you work hard enough." People who know Julie are always impressed with how hard she works. For a time, she worked as a counselor in two schools, and the two principals had not communicated with each other about what their expectations were. When Julie finally sat down with both of them at the same time, they quickly decided that they had each put too much on her plate. They had an amicable resolution to job expectation and her workload.

Julie has continued to acquire new skills and knowledge specifically for her job. She completed training from the Global Business Network (http://www.gbn.com) in a process called "Scenario Planning," which is used in some of the Academy meetings and town hall work sessions. She will tell you, however, that the set of skills that took her into the profession of counseling continue to be core components of her day-to-day responsibilities as president and CEO of the Oklahoma Academy for State Goals.

KEITH DEMPSEY

Keith Dempsey recently completed a Ph.D. in Counselor Education and works at George Fox College supervising graduate students in a master's counseling program. That's a long way from the days when Keith was a high school student at a technical high school in Portland, Oregon, where he was specializing in auto mechanics. Keith's journey has been touched by several people who have made significant interventions in his life. Perhaps chief among those was his high school track coach.

Keith described the day that his track coach pulled him out of class and handed him a paper with instructions to "fill it out." When Keith asked what it was and was informed it was a college application, he protested—"I can't afford to go to college." No one in Keith's immediate or extended family had ever gone to college. His track coach was insistent, and direct: "If you don't fill it out, then you don't run track tomorrow." Keith filled out the papers and started running in a new direction, which has resulted in a Ph.D. at present. He knows there are even more possibilities in the future.

Keith originally thought he might major in engineering but received his undergraduate degree in psychology. I asked Keith how he decided on psychology, and he answered, "I found out I liked words and people better than numbers and formulas." A job search following obtaining his undergraduate degree did not prove immediately successful in his hometown of Portland, so Keith returned to Corvallis and worked in a residential treatment facility for adjudicated youth. He said that he "wanted to know things on a deeper level" when it came to the youth, and he enrolled in a graduate program in counseling and continued working at the residential treatment center.

Throughout Keith's undergraduate and graduate years, and continuing today, is a strong desire "to give something back." He talks about the neighborhood where he grew up in northeast Portland and tells stories about the kinds of activities that have been a consistent part of his life. Keith and his Kappa Alpha Psi fraternity brothers at Oregon State University adopted a group of third-grade boys whom they continue to mentor and guide. In fact, shortly before I did the interview with Keith, he had received a cell phone call from one of the boys—now enrolled in college. The Kappa Alpha Psi brothers taught the third graders how to perform step dances and have worked with them in a variety of ways over the years. "I am a role model," Keith says, and explains the importance of models for young boys.

When I asked people what Keith brings to his work as a counselor educator, the word *passion* came up more than once. His high school track coach remembers Keith's tenacity, that he wanted to "know things," and that he wanted to be successful. The track coach commented that Keith continues to "be highly involved in his community." A former professor in his counseling program said he was "adamant about doing well," and pointed out that "he's passionate about people." A current faculty colleague of Keith's also used the word *passion,* saying that Keith is "passionate about preparing mental health professionals equipped as whole people." She also said that, "Keith puts his whole heart, soul, and life experience into what he does and his students respond to that."

When I asked Keith what counseling skills he brings to his own teaching at the graduate level, he did not hesitate and said, "All that I've done in my life and everything that I've experienced informs what I do in the classroom." That philosophy is carried out in what he tells his students: "What you have to take to your students is who you are—your person comes through in any counseling situation."

In my interview with Keith, he reflected on the persons who have been significant influences on his career path—often through a brief comment or words directed to him. He mentioned the man who lived across the street from his childhood home who spent time with him and taught him how to throw a football. Keith is sure that his mother, a single mom, was "in cahoots" with the neighbor in order to provide that influence, but says that it was significant. His track coach remains an important person. An advisor in the university's Educational Opportunity Program shocked him when he was told, "You can get a Ph.D." Keith took note of a professor who said, "You can write your own ticket." And Keith values the comments he hears from the young boys he instructed in "stepping," when they were third graders.

There have been the negative verbal influences also. We began our interview with Keith reminding me of an unsupportive comment I had made to him when he was working on his M.S. in Counseling. He had presented a request to me, program coordinator, for my approval and my words were not helpful. Keith says that the experience shaped the way he responds to his own students, making certain he does not disrespect them the same way that I had.

I asked Keith what he anticipated doing with his completed doctoral degree, and he quickly answered, "I'm doing what I want to do." It is clear that he enjoys his role as a faculty member in a counselor education program. When he talks about students, he is pleased when they can see possibilities for themselves and he feels good when he knows he has "planted a seed." My sense is that Keith has planted a lot of seeds and will continue to plant more. His continued work with at-risk youth from his own high school days on through undergraduate experiences and now as a faculty member will have a large effect on many young people. He is frank to acknowledge that, "I can't always be successful."

We ended our conversation with Keith commenting, "I have something valuable to give and I get a kick out of that." He also commented that, "The further I go on this journey, the more confident I get."

Keith Dempsey's colleagues and friends are certain that his journey will be long and profitable for many.

PEGGY HINES

Peggy Hines gets involved in a lot of system change. It has been a central theme in her academic and work experience for a number of years. At present, Peggy is the Director of the National Center for Transforming School Counseling (TSC), a major project emanating from The Education Trust in Washington, D.C. As director, Peggy oversees projects in several states where collaborative efforts of universities, school systems, and communities work together to change the way school counselors are prepared as well as the work they do. The end goal of each of those projects is to close the achievement gap observed between advantaged and other groups of students.

Peggy did not start out to be a project director at the national level. Her undergraduate preparation was in social work and radio/TV production. An internship near the end of her undergraduate studies quickly informed her that social work was not a good fit for her, and following graduation, she found her "dream job" managing an educational media center at a community college. As she says, "I helped instructors in all kinds of disciplines make their classrooms be exciting places for students to be and to learn."

Peggy started working in the public schools in a volunteer capacity when her own children were in primary grades. "I saw a lot that could be improved in public education," she said. And she credits a school counselor as the one who told her one day, "You should become a counselor."

The idea of being a counselor appealed to Peggy, and she confesses that she saw it as one way to "understand people and to control what happens to them." Understanding people is still a goal, but the control dimension has long since been replaced with other values, goals, and strategies.

Peggy had support of a spouse who encouraged her to return to graduate school for a counseling degree. Private practice was an immediate goal, and Peggy had a working relationship with a physician during and following her years in graduate school. She continued to volunteer in the schools and, at one point, had an internship with a school counselor. Peggy's orientation toward system change is illustrated in a comment she made to me in the interview: "The first day I walked in as a school counseling intern, I saw that the system had to change." That point of view and the passion to implement change carries through in her work today.

Early involvement in the Indiana School Counselor Leadership Project and with the American School Counselor Association gave Peggy a set of skills and an understanding of change strategies that had, as their objective, making systems be more effective for students rather than changing students to fit systems.

Peggy continued her involvement in professional counseling associations and gradually came to the realization that she could be in a better position to influence what happened to kids in schools and to have a broader influence on school counselors if she were in counselor education. That led to additional graduate study, an Ed.D. in Counselor Education, and an eventual position as a counselor educator. She continued to emphasize that school counselors can and should work to make systems more student friendly rather than fit students to systems—particularly when the system might be dysfunctional.

A friend's referral to a person who worked for a foundation that regularly funded educational change efforts resulted in a personal connection with a woman who was just beginning to organize efforts from The Education Trust, which ultimately resulted in the project known as Transforming School Counseling. Peggy had found a soul mate who believed that school counselors are key to making the kind of changes that benefit students.

Peggy applied for and received one of the six initial TSC projects that she implemented at Indiana State University where she held a faculty position. The funded project let the counselor education program focus on development of curriculum and process for school counselor education that had system change, social advocacy, and attention to the achievement gap as part of the core components in graduate study and in actual practice. The project also enabled Peggy to travel and be with project directors and others from across the country who were all involved in the initial stages of TSC. Her passion for seeing systems change to meet the needs of students was reinforced by the exchanges she had with the colleague group that grew around the TSC initiative.

When a position with the Education Trust opened because of the retirement of the initial director, Dr. Reese House, Peggy applied for and was hired as the new director of the National Center for Transforming School Counseling. She has continued in that position for the last 5 years. The new challenge of being employed by The Education Trust meant, among other things, that Peggy needed to find a way to manage a commuter relationship. She calls Indiana home but spends large amounts of time in Washington, DC, and in airports around the country as she works with school districts and the now 30 universities that continue with the TSC project.

Peggy's passion for helping kids has not diminished. At one point in our interview, she said, "We can't lose another kid." When I asked her about her own approach to change efforts, she thought for a moment and then responded: "There are two ways to create systemic change—either be outside and push in; or, push out from inside. My style is to join, gain trust, and work from the inside."

I asked Peggy which counseling skills from her early training she continued to use. Her quick response was, "I couldn't do my job without the counseling skills which I built in the early part of my preparation. They are a part of me; who I am." She also pointed out that in her present situation, "I'm more effective than I used to be. I used to want to control and that's not me. It's more important to work together with people to create rather than create for them. I see my job and the whole issue of system change as developing places, schools, where people can connect and work together, where the vision is to create policies and practices that ensure that every student is prepared for college and career."

I asked Peggy to reflect on her focus on being a change agent, and she responded, "There can be times where it's very lonely. When you're trying to make a place different, it isn't always the most comfortable place to be." I asked her where she gets her support in those more lonely times, and she quickly responded, "from my spouse and seeing the good things that happen to kids and from working with the people who are enthusiastic about making education institutions better places."

SCOTT CHRISTIE

Scott Christie is the Clinical Services Manager of a 20-bed addictions and mental health unit in a large hospital and medical services complex in Portland, Oregon. He reached that position from a starting point as a mental health and addictions counselor after completing an M.A. in Counseling from the University of Nevada Reno. From that clinical services beginning, Scott has moved through other clinical and program manager positions. He has been in private practice, served as the Clinical Supervisor for a crisis center in Nevada, taught violence reduction/anger management courses for men, and was an instructor for counseling and addictions courses in 2- and 4-year college settings. Scott has worked for a county mental health program as a clinician and as a clinical supervisor/manager of a county-wide addictions service delivery program.

In his present position, Scott has direct and indirect supervision of 20 staff members whose clinical and professional training cuts across medical specialties, counseling, social work, and administrative positions. Because the unit he manages is located in a comprehensive hospital complex, his direct supervisor is a medical doctor with specialty in addiction medicine, but Scott emphasizes that an essential characteristic of the group with whom he works, including an additional 20-bed psychiatric unit, is one of cooperation and collaboration with specialty distinctions minimized in the approach to patient therapy and care.

During the years that Scott worked as a mental health counselor, he continued his education and completed a Ph.D. in Counselor Education at Oregon State University. His interest in supervision coupled with work in distance education activities resulted in a dissertation examining the effects of long-distance counselor supervision using Web-based and electronic interaction for certain supervisory processes. His experience with crisis management and supervision served him well when he was hired for his present position as a program manager of clinical services in an addiction unit. He holds licenses or certificates in both mental health (Marriage and Family Therapist) and addictions (Certified Alcohol and Drug Addictions Counseling—CADC III).

In previous positions as clinician in a county mental health unit or as a manager or supervisor for a county mental health or addictions unit, Scott had to acquire specific knowledge—state administrative rules, legislative directives, regulations applying to addictions services, and organizational structures and processes in both county and state systems. He has also had to be able to work directly with legislators who were developing administrative rules that apply to mental health services and addictions counseling programs.

There have been times when Scott was responsible for developing budgets for human service programs, a knowledge and skill set he acquired after he completed his first degree. It was a form of "on-the-job" training, as he says. "I have always been confident that I could do whatever was needed in a position and could acquire the knowledge and skills to do what had to be done."

In his current position, Scott is not primarily responsible for budget development but rather budget management. Scott provides significant input to budget processes affecting the level and quality of clinical staffing, which assures patient care and program success. Scott says that the hospital has been very supportive in providing sufficient staff to get jobs done; at the same time, he knows that the hospital is a business and there is always an "eye to the bottom line."

I asked Scott about the necessary knowledge and skills to do his job as a clinical manager. His response came quickly: "You have to have a broad view of people, the system, patient care, and be open to a wide range of options in all situations." He added to the list to describe how he saw himself as a manager and administrator: "It all goes back to UPR—unconditional positive regard. I work to see the staff, the clinicians, the patients, in the most positive light."

I asked Scott what sort of thing brought him satisfaction in his job as a clinical services manager. He told me, "Seeing the staff happy and working together for the benefit of patients is great. They are a mutually supportive group who really value working together, being open with each other, valuing what each person brings to the team which has the patient's care in mind." Based on patient intake and discharge data, Scott says that the approach is working. "Patients are changing behavior, we are seeing success; and the staff enjoys being a part of that process."

As a person who entered the counseling field to be a clinician and private practitioner, I asked Scott if he missed one-on-one client contact. He answered, "I still have client contact. I can step into any treatment group and participate as a therapist, but for the most part, I rely on the staff for the clinical responsibilities while supporting their efforts. I have a great staff being successful in their work. Besides," he added, "I don't have to do case notes."

Scott is easygoing and low key. I asked him how the staff reacted to a supervisor who does not yell or holler at them and who does not make heavy demands. "They appreciate it; and I think they work harder because of it." I asked him to describe his philosophical approach to management in more detail. He answered, "I feel like a therapist—the skills are who I am and what I am. When I was working full time as a therapist, I loved it when a client had one of those 'a-ha' experiences and

I see the same thing with the staff when they see that they have choices and options about what they do." He added, "I try to maintain that non-judgmental attitude with staff. And I'll jump in and do anything with them—if a staff member is absent and they need a person to make a call or connect with a resource, I'll ask them if I can help, even if it's their responsibility. The staff enjoy their jobs; they're committed to patient care; they rely on each other; and the patients benefit."

As a manager, Scott continues to exhibit the human relationship skills that have always been a part of his makeup as a counselor. Although he says he would not have envisioned being in his present job if asked about it a few years ago, he will also say that it is a logical progression from the beginning of his counseling career to the present job. When I asked him what he saw for himself in the future and what if he was given a much larger unit to manage, he hesitated for a moment and said that he did not want to lose the opportunity to be involved with patients. "This is a big organization; I might lose some connection if I were placed in a bigger component."

TODD NOBLE

Todd Noble is the Utilization Manager for ABHA (Accountable Behavioral Health Alliance), a position he has held for 3 years. Previously, Todd worked for 14 years as a therapist, case manager, and then crisis manager in a county mental health organization.

I asked Todd about his duties as a utilization manager, and he described the frequent telephone call consultations with therapists, physicians, hospitals, emergency room physicians, and other crisis workers seeking approval for some form of treatment—inpatient or other—for persons in one of the two counties he serves. Todd also described his daily visits to mental health units in the area and explained that he had just come from the hospital. Before our conversation had finished, he received a call on his cell phone for a consultation to give approval for another patient in an adjacent county.

Todd's work puts him in hospital mental health units so frequently that he has his own keys to the local acute care psychiatric unit and, as he says, "spends more time there than many primary therapists." He added, "There's not a person who enters one of the treatment programs in these two counties under the Oregon health plan that I don't know about."

I asked Todd if he had ever considered private practice as a mental health therapist. He did not hesitate to answer that his graduate preparation program had strongly discouraged private practice and had put a heavy emphasis on doing something of social interest or for the public good rather than for personal gain. "They kind of stressed this Adlerian value of social responsibility—and that's exactly what I did." He added that he saw private practice as isolated and that there were tendencies to keep clients too long for the wrong reasons.

Todd stayed in county mental health longer than many people. He spoke with pride about developing effective protocols for assessing and treating people. He supervised a team of therapists whom he liked and said that they worked well together. Todd talked about their decisions to approach suicidality issues in a totally different manner than had been done before. "What we found was that rates hadn't changed over time even with changes in medications or in hospitalizations. We decided to shut the door to hospitalizations and develop other in-community methods of natural support." He went on to say that acute hospitalizations have their place (manic, psychotic clients), but placing suicidal clients on acute hospital wards can be counter-indicated and can be harmful.

Todd was influenced by Dr. Kurt Strosahl, a pioneer in Acceptance and Commitment Therapy (ACT). Todd's comment was that Strosahl and ACT gave them a philosophical and theoretical framework for the programs they developed. "I'm a huge client advocate. All of my passion is about doing the right clinical work. It is easy to put a person in the hospital. What you do when you do that is strip them of their dignity, take away their liberty; you demonstrate to them that they are not capable of taking care of themselves. So I have a passion to get the person in a natural system of support. I pay plenty of money for the chronically mentally ill who are disorganized, who are psychotic, who haven't slept for days, who are wandering in traffic and need to be off the street—that's what the hospital is for. But the group of people who are depressed or considering suicide need to be empowered—engaged with people."

Todd spoke enthusiastically about the work they had done in developing new assessment and treatment protocols. He continues to give talks around the state about what they developed and will soon teach a class of new medical residents on issues of suicidality. "Hospitalization is not the best way to respond to potential suicide; it takes control away from the person and is another message to them that they really aren't able to take care of themselves."

I asked Todd about the core counseling skills he brings to his work, and he answered, "I have an overriding personal value in social interest. I find meaning in life being in the helping profession. I couldn't imagine being in a job which didn't have a meaningful component in it. I have empathy for others. I'm trying to be a change agent. I'm a people person—the first criterion for a therapist is they have to be interested in people."

We talked more about approaches to therapy. Todd said, "What makes a therapist is what you bring in to it. As a little kid in elementary school, people would come to me for mediation, problem solving. In grad school, you develop the professionalism that goes along with that."

In response to a question about other professions he had considered, Todd said he had considered law school (he took the LSAT), but, "I would only have wanted to be an advocacy lawyer. I also thought about being a teacher—a history professor. I love history and listen to lectures in my car every day." Todd hopes to teach a class at the local university counseling program and is on the instructor pool waiting for an opportunity to teach.

Todd described the frustrating part of his current job. "It's a little bit isolating. I don't supervise as many people in my current job as I did in the previous job. I miss a piece of that. In my county mental health job the most frustrating thing was the continuing reduction in money and services and making everything stretch."

Todd said the most satisfying part of his work has been working with a team to get things done. "My style of management is very collaborative. I think my team [county mental health] knew I would do anything for them and they for me—they would have walked through a brick wall to do something for me and for clients. I miss some of that."

In our discussion about satisfaction in therapeutic work, Todd mentioned there is nothing tangible in most clinical work, but it is tangible in crisis work. "In crisis work, you're trying to sell hope—to get a person from point A to point B. My job was to do assessment, but I was trying to engage that person in hope; in the future; in treatment. I loved that. Hooking people; hooking them for hope."

Todd said he has no plans to change jobs in the near future. "I get to have a huge influence. I can impact policy and directly impact service to clients. The hospital has said I could go to work for them. And I've been contacted by drug companies to work for them. They said I am able to talk to physicians, psychiatrists, emergency room people, but I would rather engage clients and influence the system rather than push medications."

We talked about professionalization in mental health, and Todd mentioned that new licensing laws in Oregon will help mental health professionals. He petitioned the state which clarified state protocols for licensed professional counselors so that they are classified as being on par with other licensed professionals.

I have always been a big advocate for a counseling rather than a social work degree. Social work is a good degree, but it does not relate as much to doing therapy. Even some psychologists and psychiatrists are trained in assessment and do not have as much training in the actual therapy that they want to do. Counseling degrees could focus more on assessment, but you get that in on-the-job training. The big value of the counseling degree is the emphasis on doing therapy.

As we concluded our conversation, Todd's phone rang with a consultation call. We agreed to meet another time to continue our conversation over good coffee.

TOM EVERSOLE

"Counselor education was good preparation for work I never thought that I'd do." Tom Eversole used those words to conclude our discussion about counseling skills he has used in different professional positions. Tom's professional journey has been a rich progression of experiences.

Tom is currently the Director of Strategic Development for the College of Public Health and Human Services at Oregon State University. The steps along the path to his current position carried him through a successful practice as a veterinarian specializing in equine surgery, as a hospital orderly in a surgical unit tending persons in pre- and postoperative conditions, as a counselor (both inpatient and outpatient client service) for an HIV/AIDS project, and as a curriculum developer and trainer of trainers in AIDS prevention programs for the American Psychological Association. Prior to assuming his current position as a faculty member in a large university, he was the Director of County Health with responsibility for a full range of medical and mental health programs that employed (at various times) from 100 to as many as 140 persons in various health-related positions.

Tom describes his professional journey as a series of choices that moved him toward specializations rather than decisions to avoid either a work setting or a professional activity. Consistent throughout all his positions has been the desire to "be of service" to "see that as a result of the interaction I would have with people, their life is better than before."

College began for Tom at Virginia Tech with a degree in biology and a minor in political science. Next came veterinary school at the University of Georgia, then an internship in vet surgery at Colorado State University. He returned to the University of Georgia for a position on the faculty and a private veterinary practice. "I loved the outdoors; I loved working with horses; I loved the science of the practice." Tom maintains his license as a vet even though he has been away from the practice for a few years.

Tom's gradual move into counseling was supported by a set of different life experiences. He worked in the inner city of Baltimore in educational programs for students with chronic physical or emotional conditions. In Tom's words, "the conditions in their homes were extremely stressful—drug houses, gang activity, sex-trade districts— and I'm trying to work with a student on mathematics or European history. But I think my interactions were beneficial; you have to be where they are and work with who is there." Tom used that same approach working in a psychiatric lock-down facility for adolescents where he gained respect from the patients because he had "tackled a kid" after the much larger 18-year-old had assaulted Tom's partner—a man much bigger than Tom. "I did what I would have done if it had been a horse acting up—contain the physical violence." He went ahead to describe his office—filled with growing plants and fish tanks with an adjacent "time out" room that clients would choose to use when they knew they needed a break. "I calmly told one young man who was vocally and profanely violent in my office that "these plants want to live in a calm and peaceful world; talk like that will make them die." The young man thought for a moment and then told Tom he could handle that and continued in a calm voice.

For 3 years, Tom worked at the American Psychological Association in Washington, DC, in an HIV/AIDS prevention program. That position came after completing a master's degree in clinical psychology from Loyola College in Baltimore and an internship in an AIDS program at Johns Hopkins. That resulted in a 3-year position as a clinician in an AIDS clinic in Baltimore. When Tom's partner moved to Corvallis, Oregon, for graduate school in counselor education, Tom moved with him and continued his work for APA by telecommuting.

The intense work on AIDS prevention issues put Tom in contact with numerous people at the state level who were working on adolescent AIDS prevention issues. He assumed a larger role in managing and directing programs for delivery of service as well as educational programs on AIDS prevention for young people. It was a logical step to work in public health, and he eventually became the director of a county health program.

Client contact has always been important to Tom. As his professional career changes have taken him away from direct client contact, he has continued to find ways to be involved with persons in need and currently serves as a volunteer in a program providing beds for homeless men. He is often on site and says that he draws on all of his clinical experience to serve the men who come through the door each night.

In all his managerial, curriculum writing, client service, and organizational work, Tom continues to draw on the skill set that emerged from his counseling preparation program. "Listening to both the surface content and the deeper contextual levels is important in any setting, any position." Tom strives for transparency and honesty as a counselor, as a manager, or as a program director. "Those are skills that come from my counseling background." Working to establish good boundaries is essential in any setting. "They are critical in counseling and parallel in management. My training and experience in group work comes in to play nearly every day—my role as a facilitator is to assure that the group is a safe place. That is the same if it's a therapy group of adolescents, a group of hospital patients, or a program staff trying to devise new solutions to old problems. I have to remember that every person's statements are valid from their point of view. It is important for me to understand that point of view and to remember that the individual in a work group is like an individual in a family—it's all connected."

Tom closed our session with the words found in the first sentence of this profile: "Counselor education was good preparation for work I never thought that I'd do."

VICTORIA KANDT

Victoria Kandt is President of Victoria Kandt and Associates, a performance and executive coaching business (http://www.victoriakandt. com). She began her professional career as a first-grade teacher in a military town where the pupils represented a wide range of ethnic and economic family situations. Victoria said that she found herself spending a huge amount of time just listening to children talk about the difficult family and neighborhood situations that reflected much of life. She enjoyed teaching but felt that she could be more effective with pupils if she could work with them full time as a counselor rather than squeezing in time taken away from her teaching responsibilities.

Victoria quit her job and moved to Colorado to work full time on a master's in counseling. She supported herself with part-time work in the admissions office. Following completion of her degree, Victoria took an elementary school counseling position in a medium-sized town in Kansas. Later, she moved to a counseling position in a larger Kansas community.

Never one to be uninvolved, Victoria started giving a lot of time to the Kansas Counseling Association (KCA), eventually serving as president of the state organization. While she was working with KCA,

Victoria found herself spending a lot of time talking with other counselors—particularly new or young counselors in the field—about their work, assisting them with ideas, making suggestions about things they could do, and generally serving as a mentor to several. That mentoring (or coaching) activity was very satisfying for Victoria, and it led to her next major career step.

In a casual conversation with a friend in the business world, Victoria talked about how much she enjoyed working with the younger counselors. She described some of the mentoring activities she had been engaged in with other counselors and said it was something she would like to do on a broader scale. The friend pointed out that his company had hired a person to work with the 100 or so employees in much the same way that Victoria had said she had worked with young counselors. The friend thought the man was called "a climate counselor, or something like that." He put Victoria in touch with the internal executive coach, and the next phase of her professional life was launched.

Through conversations with the coach she had met and through another mentoring relationship, Victoria simultaneously started her own coaching company and signed up for course work from the College of Executive Coaching. This time, the career jump had more risk involved, for she moved from a school counseling position with dependable salary, paid health benefits, paid social security taxes, a known schedule, an established work routine, defined professional expectations, a colleague group, a record of good performance, retirement benefits, and job security to a field that had none of that. "It was really scary," she said in our interview.

Victoria developed a contract for services with her first client. I asked her if she had found the client on her own or if someone had referred her. She quickly explained that she had developed the contact herself. "I knew that I could do what needed to be done, but developing the contract was totally new territory for me," she said. I asked what it was like to put a price on her services and she chuckled a bit before responding, "Totally different than working as a schoolteacher or school counselor. In those positions, we never think about what our services are worth per hour for the pupils or teachers we serve. I had to put a price on the work I planned to do." Victoria said that she consulted with an attorney to develop language for the initial contract, and she consulted with some other coaches to determine a price range per hour for services. "I initially priced myself near the bottom of the range because I was so new. I think my skills and services were on a par with more experienced coaches, particularly because of my counseling degree and experience, but it was hard to name that dollar figure."

Today, Victoria's company has contracts with a number of different firms, including international companies. She travels about 1 week a month and continues to deliver about 75% of her services in face-to-face meetings; another 20% is handled by phone; and the rest is through e-mail; although, one client in Asia was entirely a phone relationship. She has a group of associates she can call in when the job requires more than one person on site at a time.

We talked about different preparation programs for coaches, about certification or licensing for coaches, and about different kinds of coaches. Victoria equated the coaching certification and licensing process to the early stages that counseling went through a few years ago. She has been guided in selecting a preparation program and in much of her work by an older person who serves as her coach. Victoria told me that most clients are less interested in the coach's certification as much as reputation. We made a short list of some of the kinds of coaches one can find, with a list of words used as adjectives to modify *coach*: They included *executive, business, personal, life, spiritual, motivational,* and *relationship.* Others could have been added.

Much of what Victoria does is similar to what she did as a counselor—she listens to clients, helps them define goals, helps them identify obstacles to goal attainment, suggests strategies to work through obstacles, and maintains contact with them through the process in order to provide support and motivation. Victoria illustrated one aspect of coaching by explaining the difference between a personal self-guided fitness program and work with a personal trainer: "I can watch an exercise program on TV and can easily decide not to do what I'm supposed to do; but when I'm in the gym with a personal trainer, I have heightened my commitment. I am paying someone to help me reach my goals; there's no way I can avoid doing what I need to do—coaching is much like that."

Victoria gets her satisfaction from seeing clients develop a place where they can really express themselves, make changes, reach goals, and accomplish what they set out to do. Her dissatisfactions come from "constantly having to market myself—something I never had to do as a schoolteacher or school counselor." She also said, "Coaching can be a lonely job." She has had recent setbacks with the downturn in the economy, finding that several companies have cut back on contracts with her kind of organization as they have implemented cost-cutting decisions. "Even if I lose a contract, I still have to pay my health insurance, my social security, my office expense, my overhead." On the other hand, she described other benefits: "If I want to take 5-day vacation to play golf, I can probably juggle my schedule to do so—I couldn't do that when I was teaching."

Victoria says she is comfortable working in a wide range of businesses now. "I don't have to know the product or the language. My expertise is in the area of their communication and their interpersonal process." The first skill set she listed when I asked about what she brought from counseling to coaching was confidentiality. "People don't understand what it's like to have confidential relationships; whereas, it has been second nature for me and is one of the first things I explain." She also listed her questioning skills, interpersonal skills, and theoretical orientation to interpersonal exchange as counseling skills she implements on a regular basis.

"I think coaching has a great future. My counselor preparation put me in a good position to move into this field and I like what I do."

JUDY FRICK

Judy Frick recently retired as the Executive Director of Communities In Schools (CIS), in Wichita, Kansas. CIS is a nonprofit organization that connects existing community services and resources with the kids and families who need them to help the kids learn, stay in school, and prepare for life. CIS provides direct services, but it also works to improve the systems that serve kids and families. CIS has grown from two staff members, a part-time secretary, and an annual budget of $150,000 in 1990, when Judy was the creating force in its start-up, to an organization 17 years later with 45 paid staff, 10 administrative staff, hundreds of volunteers, and a $1.8 million dollar budget serving 31 school sites. And now, Judy has come out of retirement to be the interim executive director while the organization searches for a new full-time director.

Judy started her professional education career teaching French in a high school in Wichita. She left that when she began a family, but enrolled in a graduate program in counseling because, "I was interested in helping people," she said in our interview. She initially thought she might become a school counselor, but a significant national conference got in her way and had a serious impact on everything else she has done in her professional life. As a representative of the Junior League in Wichita, Judy attended a conference in Baltimore, Maryland, which focused on child advocacy issues.

"For Children's Sake" was the Baltimore gathering, and speakers like Marion Wright Edelman made such an impact on her that Judy made a turn in her own professional direction and headed toward work on child welfare and child advocacy issues. She told me, "The Junior

League decided they needed to become more assertive and more action-oriented on issues about children and expand from their traditional direct service approach to an advocacy or systems change approach, and that turned me on."

Her new focus put Judy with city and state groups that had child advocacy at their core. She got involved in a group called "Kansas Action for Children" in the late 1970s and is still a member of the state board. As a member of that group, she started work collecting and presenting data to government officials, schools, and elected representatives on what needed to be done on behalf of children.

Judy said the value of her graduate degree in counseling came in to play in all of her volunteer and paid activity. "It's all about services to children, building relationships with people, finding what works, and making change. I didn't have to be adversarial in those interactions. The counseling training gave me tools for working with people." The end goal in all of her activities has been "to help kids be successful."

Communities In Schools has held conferences that have brought school and community leaders together where information and data have been presented that drives them to develop programs to assist children. Judy said, "I'm passionate about children." She also explained how gratifying it has been to be able to influence school districts, city groups, legislators, and others to take actions that benefit kids.

I asked Judy what were the strong skills she saw herself using in the years of volunteer and paid work with the many organizations listed on her résumé. She did not hesitate to say, "networking." She went ahead to explain, "Everywhere I go and everything I do involves people and I think I'm good at building networks, connecting people to information and resources and decision makers who are positioned to get things done." She laughed and told me about being in an airport just 2 days before our interview where she ran into a newspaperman she knew from Wichita. She needed to find a resource for a particular task and the newspaperman was a person who had the answer. "It's always like that," she said. "I'm always running into people and connecting them to things that need to be done."

I asked Judy what gave her the greatest pleasure in the work she has done. She did not hesitate to answer: "Networking; connections; working with a good staff at the city, state, and national levels; and all in pursuit of a worthwhile cause—kids." She was equally quick to say, "personnel," when I asked her what were the bummers in her professional career. She has been the executive director of a large organization, and managing the difficult personnel issues that normally arise is something she has not liked to do, but she pointed out that they were things that needed to be done to make the organization work effectively in pursuit of the larger goal. "It's all about kids."

As a person with a long career in a number of different organizations, it is interesting that Judy says, "I don't like conflict." Her résumé includes experiences in leadership, management, and administration. She also lists various training events she has conducted and talks about working with multiple agencies and organizations in developing grants to fund a variety of projects for kids. She has frequently been a public spokesperson for causes and actions that might not have been totally popular with everyone at the outset. It is easy to see how there might have been numerous opportunities to be in conflict with persons or agencies across the professional life span that her experience represents. Evidently her dislike of conflict was not enough to keep her away from continuing to pursue the goals related to kids.

Judy speaks with pride about being the initial organizer of the chapter of Communities In Schools in which she has invested so much of her professional life. Her résumé lists numerous honors, recognitions, tributes, and special appointments that acknowledge the significance of her work as seen by others. My guess is that there are thousands of young children who would speak directly to the value of her work in their behalf.

She closed our interview with a few comments about being an "interim" executive director for an organization that she previously headed on a permanent basis. I told her that interims had the best of all worlds—they could do what needed to be done, knowing they were soon leaving. She acknowledged that some of that was true for her. She also said that she is ready to go spend more time with her grandchildren. I imagine they are ready to spend more time with her.

ALLAN MANDELL

Allan Mandell recently moved to a new position as the Director of Community Services for Northern Nevada Adult Mental Health Services in Reno. Allan provides direct supervision for approximately 20 professionals in an organization that employs more than 500 persons, who provide service to the nearly 5000 outpatient clients in the metropolitan Reno–Sparks area. When I interviewed Allan, he was working as the Manager of Developmental Disability Services for Yamhill County in Oregon. His opening statement to me was fitting: "I always want to try new things."

Allan's career has taken him through a variety of positions—therapist, program manager, program coordinator, resource manager, and director. As a therapist, Allan has worked in one-on-one settings and in groups; he has worked in focused services such as a targeted client population in gambling addictions and with a general client population in a county mental health unit. In Allan's words, "There's always the motivation to keep going, to try something new."

Allan's graduate work was in marriage and family counseling. He said that he loved the academic climate, the intense discussions, and learning new things. His love of learning continued after he took a job with a county mental health unit in Oregon and he enrolled in a doctoral program in counselor education. At the completion of that program, he was ready to enter academia as a professor; however, as he said, "I couldn't reconcile two issues in academia—practical reality and pay." He turned down an offer of a faculty position and accepted additional administrative responsibilities in county mental health.

I observed a pattern in Allan's work history—his positions often seemed to expand in scope and responsibility as he continued with an organization. When I asked him if he moved from one level of responsibility to the next or if he took on additional responsibilities, he chuckled and admitted that the tendency was to add responsibilities rather than replace duties.

Allan spoke with pride about innovations and programs he had helped initiate in several of his work settings. As coordinator of mental health services in one county, he set up a system where people could walk in and get service immediately rather than be placed on wait lists or have services be delayed for other reasons. He said, "I decided to put together a different system for mental health. Instead of assess and refer, we set up a system where people could walk in and get service immediately. We really didn't want kids to have to go on a wait list; adults can handle that sometimes, but kids shouldn't have to."

Taking on additional tasks happens in other ways. Allan has always been interested in computers and electronic data management. He said, "When you walk in an organization and know something about computers, they think you know everything and you get responsibilities—I developed programs for work scheduling, billing, and electronic record keeping." And, typically, these functions were not part of the initial reason Allan was hired; they came as other "add-ons" in his job.

While working in county mental health, Allan created an urgent response team that streamlined evaluations and hospitalization processes. He also enhanced services by expanding the use of volunteer senior peer counselors who were trained to be more proactive with families. They helped out in a time of shrinking resources.

Allan says that he has difficulty saying "no" to the kind of requests that result in expansion of responsibilities and increased workload. In reflecting on his work history, he pointed out that he is less likely to take on overloads now. "I'm probably more realistic now. I thought I could do more than I really could. I probably had an overinflated ego."

Allan's entry to counseling was heavily influenced by the philosophy of Milan Family Therapy. He had spent a year with Josephine Mazzoli and spent additional time with her to obtain a license. Allan spent most of his time in therapeutic services, and, as he says, "I was good at it." He then became involved in domestic violence work and developed a curriculum now used with the courts which served about half of Nevada. Allan started one of the early domestic violence treatment groups for women.

In typical fashion, following completion of his master's degree, Allan took on a second job—first as a volunteer and then as a paid employee, working with Children's Behavioral Services. "I worked hard—one job from 8 to 5, then my private practice until 9, and Saturdays I would be doing domestic violence groups." Part of Allan's tendency to load up and do so much may come from his initial reason for entering the counseling field: "I got in the field in the first place to fix something and found out that I fix the most things if I can help service providers be more effective in their jobs."

I asked Allan about his counseling skills and how he applies those in the various administrative and supervisory positions he has held. He commented that he had been fortunate to hook up with great mentors. "I watched what they did and what they believed about people. I saw the social advocacy approach to people and publics and I believe that you help people when you work to change the destructive systems they are in." He spoke enthusiastically about his time and experience working with Josephine Mazzoli and continues to implement those same therapeutic skills, even in an administrative position.

Allan enjoys teaching, but other than occasional lectures or part-time teaching opportunities, he has set aside earlier career goals of being in academia. "I don't like the disconnect in academia between the academic and the real world. I love the discussions about theory, but there is a huge amount of other stuff that a person needs to know. I sought out academic training and realize that the starting point of professional practice after academic work is a place where you know you don't know what you need to know. As example, the amount of paperwork required in the real world is barely mentioned in academia. I wanted to be as good as I could be, so when I graduated with my masters, I took an additional internship so I could continue to work with good people, learn, and see what I needed to know and do. When I finished my doctorate, I would have loved academia except for the money and the demand to publish. The requirements in Public Mental Health are different."

I asked Allan what were the satisfiers in his work. He answered, "Helping someone be successful. Early on, I thought making change with one person was the goal; now, helping a counselor help a client is what I get satisfaction from." Allan told me that he thinks most of his staff (in his previous position) were pleased with the way he manages. He also acknowledged that some were not; however, based on the notes, cards, and comments he received from them, he says he thinks they appreciated what he did for them as staff.

Personnel issues are the most difficult part of his job, especially when what needs to be done (from his perspective) is constrained by union regulations or contracts. "Terminations are always hard," he said.

As we ended our conversation, Allan said, "People can make a difference in a variety of ways—with one or a hundred. The more system change you can make, the more change you make for individuals. It's not just a theory—it's just counseling." His final words were, "You can't quit; you've got to keep trying."

14

HAVE YOU FOUND YOUR WAY?

You must still be reading if you have turned to this page. This book began with the questions about your perfect career in one of the counseling professions and whether you would wait for that perfect career to find you or if you were going to seek it out on your own. It would be my hope that at this point in this book, you have a little better sense about the answers to those questions. To put it another way—"Have you found your way?"

The counseling professions are noble ventures. They are for a set of people who are willing to invest themselves in service to and for others. To many casual observers, the counseling professions appear to be an easy road. I have had people say to me, "What is hard about just listening to people?" Anyone who has worked in one of the counseling professions knows that it is hard, it takes energy, and it can be exhausting at times. It is one of those professions that is difficult to leave behind at the end of the day.

"Taking your work home with you," is an expression that many counselors will have all too much familiarity with. The sessions with a troubled young child may have ended at 1:30 in the afternoon, but the chances are good that images of the young child will be active in the head of the counselor much later in the day. I can recall my days as a school counselor, wondering if the plan that had been developed with an adolescent female would be one she could really carry out to deal with verbally and emotionally abusive parents. I confess that I was eager to hear some kind of a positive report the next day when the school doors opened.

I can also recall hearing a late-night radio newscast that named one of my former high school counselees as the person who had been arrested for shooting a police officer after wresting his gun away from him in a fight. That newscast made me think through every event and detail of our interactions at school several years before. Was there anything that could have been done differently for a young adolescent male who had some stress in his life? Could the interventions the school developed have been more effective? What would happen to a young man whom I had developed a sense of admiration for because of the difficulties he had already survived in his life?

There are many moments of satisfaction and joy in the life of a counselor. I am certain that I had more smiles than frowns when I watched the accomplishments of students. I had lots of warm feelings for the proud parents of students who watched their children reach achievements of many kinds. And I could smile, knowing that the student and I had gone through interesting conversations in my office or in the classroom or hallway. And, as is the case with counseling, neither the student nor I needed to make any public comment about what had taken place between us.

During my years as a school counselor, I can recall the very meaningful conversations with teachers—many of them new to the profession—about ways to connect with students, how to develop understanding of some of the troubled lives, and how to manage their own feelings of anger or despair about some students who seemed to be able to punch teacher hot buttons with ease. There were satisfying moments for me to able to just "be there" during teacher–parent conference times when a teacher knew he or she had an irate parent scheduled. For the teacher, having me on standby was usually enough, and after the feared conference had ended, to have the teacher say that it went really well was satisfaction enough for me.

My own journey toward finding my way began during my undergraduate days at the University of Kansas when I finally accepted the fact that public education was more appropriate for me than a career in engineering—those courses just were not much fun. The early years of teaching were filled with terrifying moments and lots of doubts about my ability to do what I had set out to do—be a teacher. Those early years also produced many satisfying moments when I was able to participate and to watch the exciting things that happen with and to young people engaged in the learning process. My own desire to keep going, to learn something new, and to do more took me on to graduate school and the study of counseling. Each new step had its own moments of doubt attached to it, but the satisfactions were also present, and I continued to be confident that I had found my way.

That "way" took me from high school teacher to school counselor to graduate student to counselor educator. It has been a good journey for me.

I tried to suggest steps you might take on your own journey. No one should consider entering the field of counseling who has not done a lot of self-examination. The exercises in the early chapters of this book have suggested just a few of the questions you might ask yourself or others in order to become aware of those aspects of who you are, which would tell you whether you are counselor material or not.

Doing an intensive look at self as part of the process of becoming a counselor can be facilitated by being a counselee. Many counselor preparation programs strongly urge and some require that students be engaged in their own counseling process before they become counselors and begin working with other people. Counselor education does not go as far as preparation in psychoanalysis, where a person is expected to be involved in his or her own analysis before and while they work with others. Asking people to go to counseling in order to be a counselor often produces interesting responses.

I have had students give me rather shocked responses that anyone would suggest they should see a counselor. Some students have said they did not need it; some have said they would go but wanted to make certain no one would know they had ever had an appointment with a counselor. This kind of response has always made me want to do a quick termination of the student. At times, I used the rejection of counseling as a focus for dialogue about what it really means to be in counseling. The typical response from persons who reject counseling for themselves is that it would be a sign of weakness or of imperfection or of not having their lives together—perhaps a great concern about other people's perception of them if the word got out that they had been to see a counselor.

I believe that rejection of the idea of counseling for yourself while purporting to want to become a counselor for others speaks volumes about how that person sees the world, how that person sees the process of counseling, and how that person would view people who go to counseling. It is difficult to imagine a counselor having much unconditional positive regard for a client when he or she would not see himself or herself as needing to be a client.

In the early chapters of this book, I said that there were very few, if any, absolutes among the list of criteria to become a counselor. I could be tempted to say that if a person does not see counseling for themselves as a benefit on the path to become a counselor, then they should step off the path and find a different occupation.

On my own journey, I found the collegial relationships with colleagues in the counseling profession to be tremendously valuable to me. Professional associations provide numerous benefits for counselors.

Those counselors who work in private or independent practice and who lead somewhat isolated lives in their practice can find particular value in gathering with colleagues for the social and professional dialogue that can happen at conventions, programs, and continuing education sessions.

I attended annual conventions of the American Counseling Association beginning with my days as a graduate student. I have never failed to return from one of those meetings without new ideas, stimulation to try new things, new colleagues with whom I have shared ideas, and good feelings from the continuing conversations with colleagues whom I see on those annual occasions. I urge all persons who are considering one of the counseling fields to find the appropriate professional association and develop ways to be engaged in the activities that will benefit them as well as their colleagues.

One excellent practice to adopt is for counselors to identify the professional journals that most closely relate to their area of special practice and then develop a regular reading habit with those journals. My own practice is to skim the table of contents of a journal the day it arrives in the mail, make a mental note of articles I want to read, then mark the page and set the journal by the chair where I do most of my reading. Because there are several journals that regularly come to the house, my stack can grow quickly, so I work to keep the most current issues at hand. This is a habit that students should develop early in their graduate study.

State licensing laws usually have requirements for counselors to accumulate a certain number of continuing education hours before they can renew their licenses. It has been my experience that people approach continuing education in one of two ways—they either grudgingly endure some education program in order to satisfy a requirement, or they eagerly participate in continuing education opportunities so as to remain fresh and current in their professional practice.

The grudging participants can often be spotted in states where all licenses renew on the same date. In the one or two months immediately prior to the time for license renewal, enrollment in continuing education workshops will shoot up. In fact, some workshop presenters count on this phenomenon and schedule their presentations in that window immediately prior to license dates knowing that enrollment will be assured. I confess that I presented continuing education workshops on that same schedule. My assumption is that counselors who wait until the last minute to obtain their continuing education hours are more inclined to enroll in anything that is available rather than in a workshop that fits their individual needs. The reluctant participants can also be spotted in the room with a rather bored look and some other activity in hand rather than the activity of the workshop. I always wonder what kind of professional counselors they might be. Are they as disinterested in their clients as they are in learning something new? Are they saying they know everything they need to know and cannot be bothered by something new or something that advances a knowledge area they already possess?

I urge you to watch for ways to be continually involved in activities that keep you fresh. Look for opportunities to be engaged with professional colleagues. It is the colleague group that best understands the stresses and strains of being a professional counselor. They are the group that does not require cautious explanation about your practice as opposed to conversations you might have with social friends who are not in the counseling business.

There is a tendency for some counselors to see graduation or licensing as the first day of their total independence. The days of instructional supervision that come with graduate school preparation are seemingly over. This is not the case. Good counselors continue with regular supervision throughout their counseling practice. The supervisory relationship is much like a good counseling relationship with respect to the kind and quality of information shared with a supervisor. The relationship should be one where a counselor can openly express doubts about self as well as be able to express confidence in action without being boastful or inappropriate. The supervisor should be able to help counselors see how their own person either gets in the way or facilitates growth with clients. Good supervisory relationships are wonderful; poor supervisory relationships are dreadful. I encourage counselors to find the supervisor who is best for them and to work hard to develop and maintain the kind of relationship that ultimately benefits clients.

A counselor's close friends, partners, and family must develop an understanding of the counselor's work. If the counselor's family has a great need to know the details of the counselor's work, then it can set up some stressful conversations. The counselor and those close need to understand that if the counselor appears distressed or distracted or worried about something, other than saying, "I'm concerned about a client," not much more will be said. "Which client?" or "What is wrong?" is the sort of question that does not get answered. It takes work to develop family boundaries about the nature of a practice.

A second kind of awkward situation for persons close to a counselor exists when a client is met at some function in the community and the client assumes that the counselor's partner or spouse knows everything that has been discussed—even after there have been extensive discussions about confidentiality. When the client identifies him- or herself as a client to a family member and then launches into an explanation of some issue out of the blue (and I have seen this happen in numerous situations), the spouse must be ready to explain that the counselor does not discuss client issues with family. Other strategies can be adopted. My spouse has had to handle situations of this kind numerous times over the years—both in person and by phone.

One of the most critical issues a counselor will have to face during his or her professional life is, "When should I get out of this business?" It does not take much questioning among members of the professional community or in communities to discover names of counselors who are judged to be ineffective. Counselors may be known who once were effective counselors but who seem to have hung on to their positions long after the time they should have left to do other things.

For private or independent practitioners, it is more difficult to know the answer to this question because they tend to practice in some degree of isolation. Counselors in larger groups or in schools or public agencies are more likely to have persons observing their work who can help them with the kind of personal assessments that say, "It's time to go." For the counselor who is still young enough that his or her normal work life is not over, leaving the counseling practice is no doubt very difficult; however, it is still one of those critical decisions that has to be made. The professional literature contains articles about impaired counselors— how to identify them and how to assist them. It is one of those touchy areas for which the profession has not found good answers.

The simple response to the question is that counselors should leave counseling when they are not effective or when there is no longer personal satisfaction and reward for what they do. The more complex response to the question is that counselors should leave counseling before they reach the point where they are no longer effective or no longer get satisfaction from what they do. Satisfaction assessments are best made by the counselor. Effectiveness assessments are best made by the counselor, the clients they serve, and the supervisors with whom they work. It takes courage for any one of those persons or groups to be able to say what they see or experience, results in their negative evaluation. This is not to say that any time a client is not satisfied the counselor should leave the profession—there will be unhappy clients as a natural part of any practice. When and what is too much? And what will you, as a practicing professional, do or say to your colleagues whom you believe to have diminished capacity? These are questions that should begin to be discussed during graduate school.

Good wishes to you wherever you are in your quest to find that perfect job. Good wishes in your studies, if that is where you are. Good wishes at the start of your practice. And good wishes as you come to the end of your professional practice and move on to the next stage of your life.

APPENDIX

PROFESSIONAL ASSOCIATIONS

Addiction Counseling Association
American Association for Marriage and Family Therapy
American Association of Christian Therapists
American Association of Pastoral Counselors
American College Counseling Association
American Counseling Association
American Marriage Counseling Association
American Mental Health Counselors Association
American Music Therapy Association
American Psychological Association
American Rehabilitation Counseling Association
American School Counseling Association
American Society for Association Executives
Association for Addiction Professionals
Association for Adult Development and Aging
Association for Assessment in Counseling and Education
Association for Clinical Pastoral Education
Association for Contextual Behavioral Science
Association for Counselor Education and Supervision
Association for Counselors and Educators in Government
Association for Creativity in Counseling
Association for Lesbian, Gay, Bisexual, and Transgender Issues
   in Counseling

Association for Multicultural Counseling and Development
Association for Pastoral Counseling and Supervision
Association for Play Therapy
Association for Rational Emotive Behavior Therapy
Association for Specialists in Group Work
Association for Spiritual, Ethical, and Religious Values in
    Counseling
Association of Oncology Social Work
Association of Professional Consultants
Clinical Social Work Association
Counseling Association for Humanistic Education and
    Development
Counselors for Social Justice
Institute of Management Consultants
International Association of Addictions and Offender Counselors
International Association of Coaching
International Association of Marriage and Family Counselors
International Coach Federation
International Family Therapy Association
National Association for College Admission Counseling
National Association of Addiction Treatment Providers
National Association of Lesbian and Gay Addiction Professionals
National Association of School Psychologists
National Association of School Social Workers
National Association of Social Workers
National Career Development Association
National Christian Counselors Association
National Employment Counseling Association
National Staff Development Council
Psychologists in Independent Practice
School Social Work Association of America
Society of Clinical Child and Adolescent Psychology
Society of Clinical Psychology
Society of Consulting Psychology
Society of Counseling Psychology

INDEX

A

Abuse reports, 51, 74
ACA, 123, 134, 136, 164
Acceptance and Commitment Therapy
    (ACT), 148
Accountable Behavioral Health Alliance
    (ABHA), 147, 149
ACEG, 93–94
ACT, 148
Addiction counseling
    from call centers, 90
    certificates for, 95, 145
    by Christie, 145
    funding for, 46, 95
    issues related to, 95
    on military installations, 94
    Smith on, 135
    12-Step model for, 95
    Web searches for, 65
Administration, school, 59–60, 128–130,
    135
Advanced Management Program,
    126–127
Aggressive behavior, 34
Alcoholics Anonymous, 20, 95
Allen, Evelyn, 130–133
American College Counseling
    Association, 59

American College Personnel
    Association, 59
American Counseling Association
    (ACA), 123, 134, 136, 164
American Mental Health Counseling
    Association, 134
American Psychological Association,
    150, 151
American Red Cross, 134–135
American Rehabilitation Counseling
    Association (ARCA), 93, 96
American School Counselor
    Association, 59, 143
Analyze This (movie), 71
ARCA, 93, 96
Assertiveness, 34
Assistantships, 40
Association for Counselors and
    Educators in Government
    (ACEG), 93–94

B

Background information sheets, 72
Banks, 70
The Bob Newhart Show (television show),
    71
Boundaries, maintenance of, 29–30, 34,
    165–166
Budgets, 146

171